AMERICAN FLY TYING MANUAL

Dressings, and methods for
tying nearly 300 of America's
most popular patterns

Dave Hughes

Photos by: Andrew E. Cier

Illustrated by: Richard Bunse

All flies tied by Randy Stetzer

FRANK AMATO PUBLICATIONS
P.O. Box 82112, Portland, Oregon 97282
(503) 653-8108

About the Author

Dave Hughes is a professional writer and amateur aquatic entomologist. He started fly fishing before his teens. He started tying flies soon thereafter because his father couldn't tie them as fast as Dave could lose them. That was nearly thirty years ago.

Dave has taught fly tying classes for several years through Clatsop College in Astoria, Oregon. His articles about fly fishing and fly tying have been published in *Flyfishing, Salmon Trout Steelheader, Fly Fisherman, The Fly Fisher, Rod & Reel, Field & Stream, Outdoor Life,* and The Scientific Anglers *Handbook.* Among his articles is one titled, "Teaching Fly Tying," directed not to tiers but to those who teach fly tying. It appeared in *Fly Tyer,* where Dave has had a regular column.

Long a popular lecturer at conclaves and club banquets, Dave is a charter member of the Rainland Fly Casters, a member of Trout Unlimited, and was founding president of Oregon Trout. He received the 1985 Lew Jewett Memorial Life Membership award from the Federation of Fly Fishers.

Dave was born and raised in Astoria, Oregon. He lives there now.

Other books by Dave Hughes: *The Complete Book of Western Hatches* (with Rick Hafele), *An Angler's Astoria, Western Fly Fishing Guide, Western Streamside Guide, Handbook of Hatches, Reading The Water,* and *Tackle and Technique for Taking Trout.*

JIM SCHOLLMEYER

About the Book

American Fly Tying Manual is both an introduction to the art of fly tying, and an advanced work that lists 290 of the most popular and useful fly patterns.

Ten percent of the fishermen are said to catch ninety percent of the fish. The 290 flies listed in this book are the ones those top ten-percenters use most of the time, to catch most of their fish, all across the continent, for all kinds of fish: trout, bass and panfish, salmon and steelhead, even saltwater fish.

If you have never tied flies, the *American Fly Tying Manual* will teach you how, from tying the thread on the bare hook to cementing the head of your finished fly.

If you already tie your own flies, the *American Fly Tying Manual* will cut through the confusion of the thousands of fly patterns that have been devised through the centuries. It will help you select those flies that really catch fish. Your fly boxes will be organized, and they will always contain the flies that you need without being so cluttered with odds and ends of flies that you can never find the one you want.

Each fly is shown in full color, so that you can tie it exactly as it should be tied, with proper proportions, and the correct colors. The dressing for each fly is given in detail, and in the order that each material is tied onto the hook.

Step by step directions are given for tying dry flies, wet flies, nymphs, streamers, and salmon/steelhead flies. From the close-up photos of each step, you will quickly learn to tie all of the flies listed in the book.

Table of Contents

Copyright 1986 Dave Hughes • Book Design: Joyce Herbst
Second Edition 1989
Printed in Canada ISBN: 0-936608-45-5

Chapter 1

Anatomy of an artifical fly

An artificial fly is built on the backbone of a hook. A variety of materials are used to flesh it out to the desired form. These include furs, feathers, tinsels, hairs, chenilles, yarns, and a new and growing array of synthetics. The desired form of a fly is based on something a fish would normally eat, or something a fish might want to eat. But the form is not always based closely on a natural food.

Some flies are tied as *attractor* flies. These use flash or color to attract fish, giving them the idea that here is something that might be good to eat, or inciting them to attack and strike the fly out of anger or some other mysterious motivation.

Other flies are tied as *searching* flies. These resemble in a general way many of the food forms that fish eat. They are selected to be rough estimates of the average size, color, and shape of the general run of food for the specific species you are after. If your quarry is trout, you might select a small, drab nymph for its resemblance to many aquatic insects. If you are after tarpon, you would likely select a great streamer to suggest a range of saltwater baitfish.

Some flies are tied as *exact imitations* of a specific food type. These are used when fish feed exclusively on one type of organism, and you have a choice of matching it closely or catching no fish. For trout, exact imitations are usually tied to match a particular species of aquatic or terrestrial insect. For bass, they commonly take the form of frogs, leeches, mice, or minnows. For saltwater fish, imitations are usually tied to reflect shrimp, sand eels, and baitfish.

All fish are most comfortable feeding on what they've become accustomed to eating in the past, just like us. But some fish are more aggressive than others, and more willing to try something new. Trot an exotic invention past the nose of a predaceous bass and it is most likely going to take a swipe at it. Retrieve something new and alarming past the nose of a trout and it is more likely to flee from it. Trout typically feed on smaller organisms, and often feed selectively. They are therefore more likely to require that your flies resemble the size, form, and color of what they're accustomed to eating before you will catch them.

Size, form, and color are the aspects of a fly that a tier varies to make it resemble the desired food. Size is varied simply by choosing different sizes of hook. Form is varied by selecting the kind of materials that go on the hook, and the way they are tied on it. Color of the fly is varied, of course, by changing the colors of the materials used. It has often been said that these three variables are important in a particular order; for example, size, form, then color. But a fly that is far off in any of the three can cause a fish to turn away. A good tier is aware of all three aspects.

The form of a fly must always follow the function of a fly: materials must be chosen based on the way you will fish the fly. It would not be very productive to tie a wet fly or streamer with stiff materials that refuse to work and move in the water when the fly is retrieved. On the other hand, it wouldn't do much good to tie a dry fly out of soft materials that soak up water and cause the fly to sink. When selecting materials for a fly, always consider where and how that fly is designed to be fished.

HOOKS

The hook is the backbone of the fly; it is also your connection to the fish. Hook numbering can confuse you if you let it. But it can also be simple if you learn a few basic facts.

Hook size (Illustration 1) is simple: from size No. 1, hooks get smaller as their number gets larger, and from size 1/0, hooks get larger as their number gets larger. Thus a No. 2 hook is larger than a No. 12, and a No. 6/0 is larger than a No. 2/0.

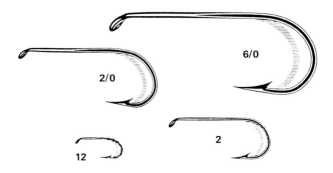

Illustration No. 1

Hook eye styles (Illustration 2) are also simple. The turned up eye (TUE) is used for steelhead and salmon flies and some types of dry flies. The straight or ringed eye (RE) is used for midges, some streamers, and for saltwater flies. The turned down eye (TDE) is the most commonly used kind; it is the one you will find on 90% of the flies you buy commercially. The tapered eye makes a lighter hook, and is used for dry flies. The ball eye is slightly heavier and is used for wet flies and streamers. The looped eye is used on steelhead and salmon hooks, because it is strongest.

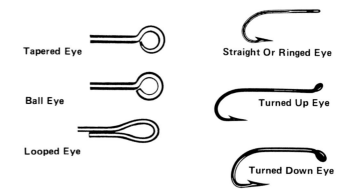

Tapered Eye

Ball Eye

Looped Eye

Straight Or Ringed Eye

Turned Up Eye

Turned Down Eye

Illustration No. 2

Hook bends (Illustration 3) are mostly a matter of eye appeal, though there are endless debates about the hooking qualities of each kind. The Viking, Sproat, and Limerick are the three most popular styles; they've all been around for years, and they all hook and hold fish well.

Wire weight and hook length are two very important aspects of the hook. If you want a fly to fish wet, you want a stout-wire hook; if you want it to fish dry, you want a fine-wire hook. If you are imitating a long and slender insect, you want an extra-long hook shank; if you are imitating a short, stout one, you want an extra-short shank.

The gap on a certain size hook, say a No. 8 (Illustration 4) always stays the same. But the hook may vary in length from 5 extra-short to 8 extra-long. Each X means the hook shank is shortened or lengthened to the standard length of a hook one size larger or smaller. For example, a 2X long No. 8 hook has a No. 8 gap and a No. 6 shank length. A 2X short No. 8 hook has a No. 8 gap and a No. 10 shank length.

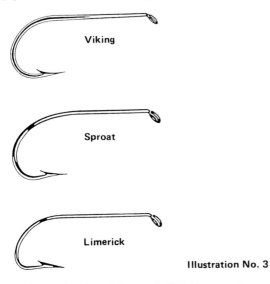

Viking

Sproat

Limerick

Illustration No. 3

The same applies to hook weight: each X designates the hook wire is heavier or lighter to conform to the standard wire of a hook one size larger or smaller. For example, a 2X fine No. 8 hook would be made from the same wire as a standard No. 10 hook. A 2X stout No. 8 would be made from the wire of a standard No. 6 hook.

Gap/Length Combinations for a Typical No. 8 Hook

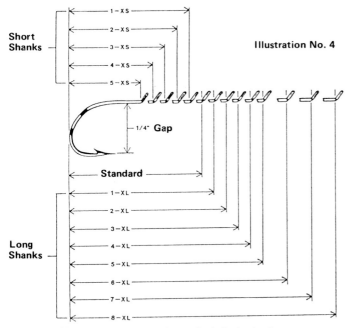

Short Shanks

1 – XS
2 – XS
3 – XS
4 – XS
5 – XS

Illustration No. 4

1/4" Gap

Standard

Long Shanks

1 – XL
2 – XL
3 – XL
4 – XL
5 – XL
6 – XL
7 – XL
8 – XL

Note: Measurements do not include the hook eye.

There are a few hook numbers that are the standards of the industry. Most beginning tiers start with these few hooks; most experienced tiers, and most professional tiers, still use them.

Dry fly: Mustad 94840. Standard length, TDE, 1X fine wire.

Wet fly: Mustad 3906. Standard length, TDE, standard wire.

Nymph: Mustad 3906B. 1X long, TDE, standard wire.

Streamer: Mustad 9672. 3X long, TDE, standard wire.

Salmon/steelhead: Mustad 36890. 2X long, looped TUE, standard wire, black.

THREADS

If a hook is the backbone of a fly and materials are its flesh, then thread is the tendons that hold it together. Threads can be as complicated as you please, for there are many different kinds on the market. But they can also be very simple, because all of your tying can be done with just two spools.

The first thread you need is 3/0 monocord (pronounced three-ought). This is a stout thread that ties flies down to size 12 or even 14 if you are stingy with the number of wraps you take. It's a good thread to learn with because it won't break all the time and drive you crazy while you are learning to be light-handed. Monocord comes in a wide range of colors, and it is available either waxed or unwaxed. The beginner should start with a spool of black waxed 3/0 monocord.

The second thread you need, and the one you will do most of your tying with when you get used to it, is 6/0 nylon. This is a much finer thread, and obviously better when you progress to the tying of smaller flies. It builds up less bulk with the same number of wraps, tying a neater fly. It is a strong thread for its diameter, and you will use it for both small and large flies as soon as you learn to use it without breaking it. The finer thread makes for a neater fly, even on a large hook diameter. The 6/0 nylon comes in any color you will want, and is available waxed or unwaxed. Waxed is a bit easier to work with. Again, the first color you will want is black.

There are other threads for specific purposes; 3/0 monocord and 6/0 nylon will tie your flies until you encounter a specific need.

BODY MATERIALS

The body of a fly is a lot of what makes it look like something good to eat, to a fish. A variety of materials are used to construct bodies. Some are selected because they give an impression of the real thing and also move enticingly in the water. Various animal furs and synthetic furs are in this category. They are by far the most popular materials for fly bodies. Other materials are selected because they make bodies that look exactly like the real thing. These are generally hard materials: hackle stems or latex or flat synthetics like Swannundaze. They gain in realism, but one must remember that they usually sacrifice lifelike movement.

Furs such as Australian opossum, beaver, badger, mole and muskrat are usually used in their natural colors. And remember that the color varies from belly to back, getting darker as you go up and around. An English hare's mask and ears has several shades of tan and brown dubbing fur, which is used for what might be America's most popular nymph: the Gold Ribbed Hare's Ear.

Seal fur is a bright-fibered body material, usually used in dyed colors for steelhead and salmon flies. African goat, also dyed in a wide array of colors, is a good substitute for the expensive seal.

The advent of dying has made it possible to attain all the various shades of the natural foods of fish. It has made another thing possible: you can now buy one kind of fur in the colors you are most likely to need, keep it organized in the packages it comes in, and cut down the clutter on your fly tying bench and in your mind. I have a fur file that contains 36 colors of Hare-Line and Hare-tron dubbings. With that I have the spectrum of colors covered, and seldom have to reach for anything else. Fly-Rite is another product, made of polypropylene synthetic, available in all popular colors.

Wool yarn is also used for fly bodies. It is best for wet flies and nymphs because it soaks up water.

Antron is a new synthetic yarn that sparkles in the water.

It can be used alone, or chopped and blended with natural furs to give an extra spark of life.

Chenille is a body material that comes in most colors, and makes a fine, fat, buggy body. It is most famous for its use in the Woolly Worm.

Latex is a modern dental product; it is cut in strips and wound as the body for caddis larva imitations. Swannundaze is a flattened, flexible nylon strand that is used as ribbing for nymphs, or even as the whole body on some flies. It gives a bold segmented effect.

Tinsel is the most popular material for ribbing flies. It gives flash, helping to attract fish. It is generally used in gold and silver. It can be flat, oval, or round. Flat tinsel can be plain, or embossed with a pattern that helps it reflect light. The most popular tinsel today is Mylar tinsel. It is virtually unbreakable, and comes gold on one side and silver on the other, so that one spool does it all.

Gold, copper, and silver wire are also used for ribbing on small flies.

Herls from the feathers of large birds are often used as bodies. Peacock is the most popular; it makes a body that has a special olive color, and that reflects tiny points of light. Pheasant tail, from the ringneck rooster, is also popular, and makes the famous Pheasant Tail Nymph, and also the Teeny Nymph. Ostrich is still called for in many patterns. In the past there have been many dressings that called for crow, raven, turkey, condor, and other kinds of herls. These are less common today.

Lead wire, generally chosen to be the same diameter as the wire of the hook, is used to weight nymphs.

HACKLES

Hackles can be divided into two types by their primary uses: dry fly hackles, and sunk fly hackles. Hackles for drys should be stiff, shiny, and web-free. Hackles for wets, nymphs,

and streamers should be softer, and can have quite a bit of center web to absorb water.

Dry fly hackles come from the necks of rooster chickens, graded No. 1 or No. 2. The original source was from fighting cocks. Then tiers turned to imported necks from India and China. Now the fly tying market is so strong that domestic chickens are genetically chosen and carefully raised specifically for the hackle market. Good domestic necks are the most expensive; they are also usually the best bargain.

Saddle hackles come from just in front of the rump of the rooster. They are used to tie larger dry flies, although some growers are beginning to produce saddle hackles in smaller sizes. I have a Henry Hoffman Super Grizzly saddle patch that ties tiny No. 18 and 20 flies. Saddles are also used for streamer wings.

Wet fly hackles are generally from hen necks, or grade 3 rooster necks. Feathers from the wings and bodies of many land birds are also used for wet fly hackles; these include partridge, grouse, starling, and snipe.

A list of the most commonly used colors of hackles:

Brown: Also called Brown Red Game.
Coachman brown: Very dark brown.
Badger: White or cream with a black center stripe.
Furnace: Brown on the edges with a black center stripe.
Blue dun or dun: Gray with a bluish cast; light, medium, and dark.
Ginger: Light to medium tan.
Ginger variant: Tan with indistinct brown markings.
Grizzly: White and black barred.
Variant: Any color with indistinct patterning of another color.

WINGS AND TAILS

The most popular traditional wing material is paired sections from the flight feathers of mallard wings. These are listed as "quill," though outside the fly tying world the term quill would naturally apply to the stem of the feather. Turkey, grouse, and pheasant quill sections are also used for winging.

Flank feathers, located on the body of the bird at the base of the wings, are also used as both wet and dry fly wings, and as tails. The most popular is the lemon-colored wood duck flank feather, which can be substituted for with a lemon-dyed mallard flank feather. Teal and pintail flank feathers are also used at times, as is the mallard breast feather.

Marabou might make the best, most active, streamer wings available, and it is also used for tails, and as wingcase material on some nymphs. It comes dyed in any color you could want.

Hollow deer and elk body hair might make the best dry fly wings for rough-water situations. Deer hair is used on such popular patterns as the Humpy and the Grizzly Wulff. Elk hair, little used in the past, has suddenly become very popular with the advent of a killing little dry fly, the Elk Hair Caddis. But the most popular winging material for hairwing flies is probably white calf tail, largely because it is so visible. Calf tail is also the most popular hair for steelhead fly wings.

Longer hairs, such as bucktail in white and brown, is used as wings on bucktail flies, and also as tails and wings on some of the larger dry flies. Arctic fox, red fox, and gray fox tails are all used to wing streamers and steelhead and salmon flies. Arctic fox fur has a naturally graceful action when wet and retrieved through the water.

Squirrel tail hair, from both the gray and red fox varieties, is used a lot as tailing material, and also as downwings on stonefly and some caddisfly dressings. Woodchuck hair is especially popular for wings on dry caddis patterns.

FLY TYING TOOLS

You can judge a fly tier by his tools. Although you don't need to spend a great deal of money to get started in fly tying, it is wise to spend your money where it will do the most good. Don't try to save money on the five basic tools.

The Five Basic Tools:

1. The vise you choose should be adjustable for height, and should have an adjustable clamp so that you can fasten it to a wide variety of surfaces. It should have tapered, adjustable jaws that hold hooks at least from No. 20 to No. 2. A Thompson Model A, or one of very similar description and quality, will serve you well for years.
2. Your scissors should have fine points so that you can clip in close quarters with deadly accuracy. They should have stiff blades that do not bend and open when faced with a stiff material, such as the stem of a large hackle. They should have large finger holes; eventually you will tie with your scissors on your fingers, never setting them down.
3. A good bobbin has a fairly long barrel that is smooth, and doesn't fray or cut your thread. It is made of good steel, so that it can be adjusted to put the proper tension on your thread spool. It should be adjusted so that the spool surrenders thread when you roll it with your thumb, and never rolls when the spool is just hanging.

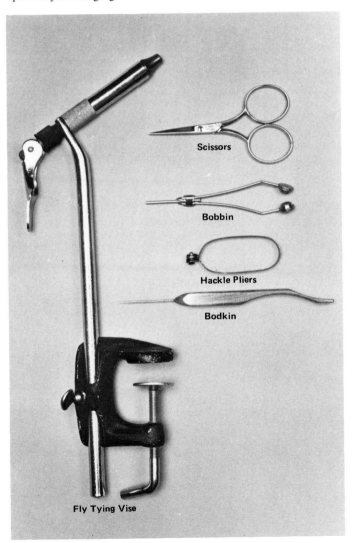

Scissors

Bobbin

Hackle Pliers

Bodkin

Fly Tying Vise

4. The best hackle pliers for most tying are Thompsons, with one rubber jaw, one serrated steel jaw. Their great advantage

for a beginning tier — or an experienced tier, for that matter — is that they don't have sharp jaws which cut the hackle tip, the biggest problem with metal-jawed pliers.
5. Most anything will do for a bodkin: a needle stuck in a wooden match or a biologist's dissecting needle. It is used to apply head cement to the finished fly, and to pick out materials that are accidentally wound under the thread.

Other Useful Tools:

There are many other tools that you will find useful, but that you can do without if you have to. The first of these is a whip finish tool, which will make your finished flies much neater and a lot more durable. A bobbin cleaner and threader makes it easier to use waxed threads, and to change thread colors. A hair stacker can be used to even the tips of hairs such as deer, elk, and bucktail so that the tails and wings you tie with these hairs are straight and even. Bees wax or Wonder Wax will make it easier to spin dubbing on your tying thread.

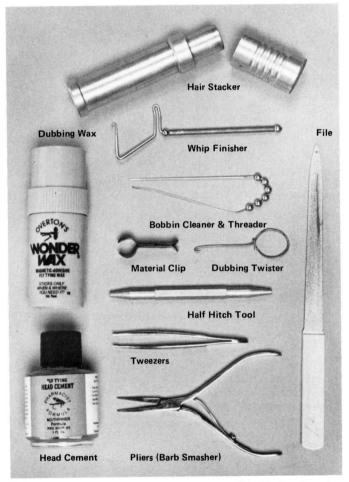

Hair Stacker

Dubbing Wax

Whip Finisher

File

Bobbin Cleaner & Threader

Material Clip **Dubbing Twister**

Half Hitch Tool

Tweezers

Head Cement **Pliers (Barb Smasher)**

A materials clip attached to your vise will hold tinsels and chenilles out of the way until you are ready to wind them on the fly. A dubbing twister will serve when you want to make a tight fur body on a loop of your working thread. A half-hitch tool can be used to finish your fly if you won't want to spend the extra money for a whip finish tool. A pair of tweezers can be used to police up stray fibers of hackle and fur after the fly is finished. Head cement is used to give the head of the fly a finished appearance, and to keep the head of the fly from unraveling.

A small pair of pliers should be kept on your tying bench to de-barb your hooks, and an inexpensive diamond fingernail file is the best thing I have found to sharpen a hook. A sharp hook without a barb will catch more fish than a dull hook with one.

Chapter 2

Learning to tie flies

To tie well you've got to have a tying area where you can be comfortable. Your table or desk should have plenty of room to spread out tools and materials. If its surface is not light in color, then get a 2' by 2' sheet of light green matt paper from a framing shop, and clamp this under the vise. It will prevent eye strain. A good light source should be directed at the fly, not into your eyes. The vise should be set at a comfortable height, about seven to eight inches, and placed so it holds the hook right in front of you.

The bobbin should be adjusted so the thread spool turns just before the thread breaks. It can be adjusted by removing the spool and bending the wire legs slightly in or out to increase or decrease tension.

Scissors, bobbin, hackle pliers, and bodkin should be placed to the right (if you are right handed) of the vise within easy reach. Materials for the fly being tied should be laid out in the order they will be tied on to the fly. Keep clutter and confusion to a minimum.

Each new pattern should be read carefully before you begin to tie it. Materials should be listed in all patterns in the order in which they will be tied onto the hook.

The first thing you should do when setting up to tie flies for the first time is learn to break your thread. Put it in the bobbin, wrap it around the hook, then pull until it breaks. Do this several times. There is no better way to learn that fine line between using enough tension to hold materials firmly in place, and using too much tension and breaking the thread.

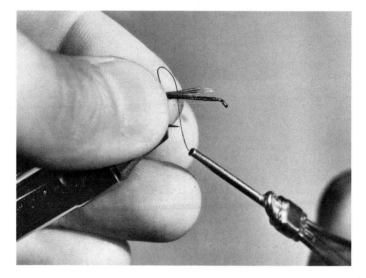

Using a Soft Loop

The next thing to do is learn to tie the *soft loop*. This enables you to tie materials exactly on top of the hook rather than rolling them off to the side. To use the soft loop, hold your material where you want it on the hook shank, between thumb and forefinger. Then slip the thread up between your thumb and forefinger and back down between them on the other side of the materials and the hook. Leave a 1/4-inch loop above the hook. Keep your thumb and forefinger pressed together so that the thread loop is held between them, straight over the hook and materials. Now bring the bobbin barrel under the hook and pull *straight toward you* while allowing the loop above the hook to slip down onto the materials, locking them into place. *The soft loop will be used nearly every time you tie something onto a hook.*

Learn to use your fingertip, or a half hitch tool, to roll a half hitch onto the head of the fly. Just make a loop around the end of your finger and put your finger to the hook eye. Now slip the loop off your finger, urging it with your thumb if that helps, and over the eye, directing it into place with your fingertip. You will use three or four half hitches to finish the heads of your flies until you learn to tie a whip finish.

This is a good time to buy a whip finish tool and learn to use it. A whip-finished head will be neater and hold better than one finished with half hitches. See page 16 for instructions on how to tie a whip finish without a tool.

Making a Half Hitch

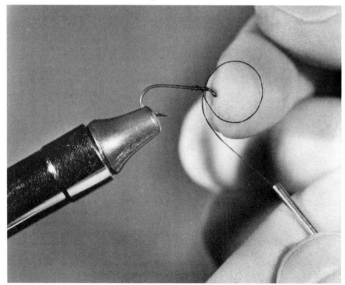

Introduction to Dry Flies

Most dry flies represent aquatic insects that have just emerged from under the water, or that have returned to the water to lay their eggs. Others represent insects that have fallen to the water from land; these are called terrestrials.

Dry flies must float, and they must be visible to you if you are to detect the take of a fish. The more hackle a dry fly has, the bushier it is, and the higher it floats. Drys designed to fish in rough water have two and sometimes three hackle feathers wound on them. Those for less turbulent water are tied more sparsely, with just five or so turns of hackle. Some drys, designed for calm stretches of rivers and for lake fishing, have no hackle at all, floating on the support of the tails, body, and wings. These are the most exact imitations of natural insects.

Materials for dry flies should repel water. Select stiff fibers for the tails, water repellent furs such as muskrat for the bodies, and use stiff, web-free hackles. Many wise tiers dress their dry flies with floatant as soon as they finish tying them. Some rub floatant into body fur before they wind it onto the hook. This treatment keeps dry flies floating a lot longer than a coating of floatant applied just before the fly hits the water.

Various Types of Dry Flies

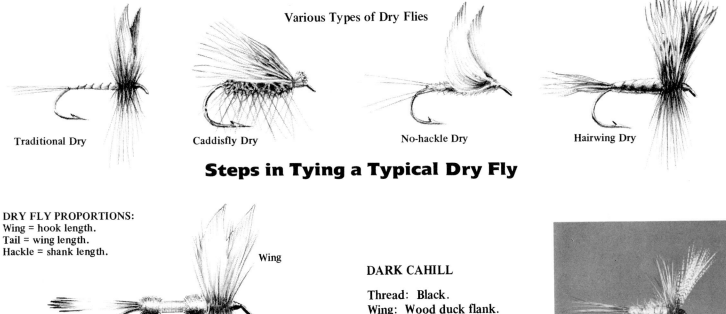

Traditional Dry   Caddisfly Dry   No-hackle Dry   Hairwing Dry

Steps in Tying a Typical Dry Fly

DRY FLY PROPORTIONS:
Wing = hook length.
Tail = wing length.
Hackle = shank length.

Wing

Tail   Body   Hackle

DARK CAHILL

Thread: Black.
Wing: Wood duck flank.
Tail: Brown hackle fibers.
Body: Muskrat body fur.
Hackle: Brown.

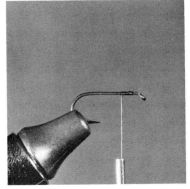

1. Clamp a size 10 hook in the vise so the jaws cover the bottom half of the hook bend. Cradle the bobbin in your right hand (left if you are left handed) and hold the thread tip with your left thumb and forefinger. Near the eye of the hook, take two wraps forward, then lay a base of thread wraps back over 1/4 of the hook shank. Trim excess thread.

2. Align the tips of a wood duck flank feather. Strip from the stem those fibers on each side that do not come out even. Holding the feather between left thumb and forefinger, measure it the length of the whole hook. Move it forward to a point 1/5th of the hook shank behind the eye. Using a soft loop, tie it in there with five to eight firm wraps.

3. Stand the wing upright with your left thumb and forefinger. Take a few wraps directly in front of it to hold it upright. Divide the wing in half, then alternately hold each wing tip while you take two figure eights of thread between them to hold the wings apart. Cut the excess wing feather stem half way to the hook bend.

4. Lay a base of thread wraps to the hook bend. Select ten to 20 stiff fibers from a brown hackle. Extend these straight out from the stem so the tips are even, then strip them away from the stem. Measure them the length of the wing and tie them in at the hook bend with a soft loop and five to eight firm wraps.

5. Cut a small clump of muskrat fur from the hide. Pull out the long guard hairs. Tease the fur into a two-inch skein, tapered at both ends. Wax your thread well. Now hold the fur against the thread and twist it, in only one direction, onto the thread. Twisting in both directions tightens and then loosens it again each time. Strive for a neat taper on the thread.

6. Wrap the body to the base of the wing, striving for an even taper back to front, with no gaps or lumps. If you come out with extra fur, remove it from the thread. Add more if you come out short. It will take some practice before you can calculate the right amount of fur each time, for each hook size.

7. Select two hackles with fibers the length of the hook shank. Peel the webby fibers from the lower ends. Hold the hackles back to back, lay them on top of the hook shank with the tips over the tail and the stems between the divided wings. Tie them in with two wraps behind the wings, five to eight in front. Clip the excess stems well behind the hook eye.

8. Grasp the tip of the far hackle with your hackle pliers. Wrap three turns of hackle behind the wings. Cross to the front under the hook and take two or three turns in front of the wings. Tie off the hackle tip with three to four wraps, and clip excess. Be sure you are leaving room for the fly head. Do the same with the other hackle, winding it over the first one.

9. Hold the hackle back out of the way with your left thumb and forefinger. Use wraps of thread to fill the gap where the hook wire meets the hook shank — this can cut your leader. Now build up an even, tapered head. The biggest problem most first-time tiers have is not leaving sufficient room for the head. Discipline yourself to keep things back a bit.

10. Use the tip of your forefinger or a half hitch tool to seat three or four tight half hitches at the back of the head, just in front of the hackle. This is the place to use your whip finish tool if you have one. Place a drop of cement on the head with your bodkin. Clear the hook eye by running an excess hackle tip through it. Contemplate the finished fly!

Introduction to Wet Flies

Wet flies represent drowned adult aquatic insects, or terrestrial insects, or nymphs of aquatic insects rising to the surface to emerge into the adult stage. Many of them are also tied just to look like something good to eat, with a bit of flash and color. These are *attractors*.

Wet flies are usually fished just beneath the surface, seldom more than a few inches deep. They are not often weighted, but they are almost always tied with materials that absorb water.

The best hackles for wet flies come from birds with soft feathers: hen necks, rooster necks that are not good enough to be dry fly quality, and such land birds as grouse and partridge. Body materials may come from animals that do not swim, thus do not have water repellent fur. Rabbit is excellent, and comes in a wide range of dyed colors.

Various Types of Wet Flies

Traditional Wet Fly   **Soft-hackled Wet Fly**   **Woolly Worm**

WET FLY PROPORTIONS:
Tail = shank length.
Hackle = shank length.
Wing = midpoint of tail.

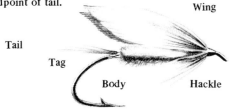

Tail

Tag

Body

Wing

Hackle

Steps in Tying a Typical Wet Fly

LEADWING COACHMAN

Hook: Mustad 3906, No. 8-14.
Thread: Black.
Tag: Medium silver tinsel.
Tail: None.
Body: Peacock herl.
Hackle: Coachman brown.
Wing: Mallard quill.

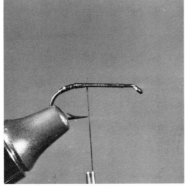

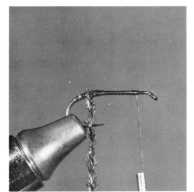

1. Place a size 8 or 10 hook in the vise. Start your thread just behind the hook eye, and wrap adjacent wraps all the way to the hook bend, laying a firm base for the rest of the fly. This firm base, used on almost all flies, keeps materials from sliding around the hook after the fly is tied. Trim the excess thread.

2. Tie in about three inches of flat tinsel where the hook begins to bend. If you use mylar tinsel, tie it in with the silver side to the hook; when you wrap it on it will then have the silver side out. Take three or four wraps of tinsel down the bend of the hook shank and the same number back over them to the hook bend. Tie off and trim excess.

3. From a peacock eyed tail feather, select four or five herls that are the same length. Pull or cut them away from the stem. Tie them in by the tips, with gentle wraps. Form a loop of thread the length of the herls, using your left index finger, and secure the base of the loop with four to five wraps of thread. Wrap thread to hook eye and trim excess herl tips.

4. Grasp the loop end and the herl butts between your thumb and forefinger. Twirl them until they form a herl rope. Be careful not to wind them up so tight that the herls break where they are tied in. You can now attach your hackle pliers to the end of the rope, or you can hold the tip of the rope in your fingers to perform the next step.

5. Using the hackle pliers or your fingers, wrap a herl body to a point 1/5 of the hook shank behind the hook eye. You will find it necessary to twist the rope again as you go. Tie off with five or so wraps, and clip excess. You now have a body that is naturally tapered from back to front, and that will stay together no matter how many fish chew on it.

6. Select a hen or soft rooster hackle feather with fibers the length of the hook shank. Remove the fluffy fibers from the bottom of the stem. Tie in with five to eight wraps, being sure the concave side of the feather is toward the hook shank. Clip excess stem. When tying any fly take just those thread wraps that are needed. This prevents build-up of too much bulk.

7. Grasp the hackle tip with the hackle pliers. Take three or four wraps of hackle just in front of the body. Tie off the hackle and clip the excess tip. With the thumb and forefinger of your left hand, hold the hackles back while you take three or four wraps against the front of them, to hold them swept back. This also takes care of fibers that were caught under the thread.

8. Select matched mallard primary feathers from a left and right wing. Clip a section from each about 1/8 inch in width. Meld these, with concave sides together, so that their tips are even. The sections in the middle and the butt of the feather are softer and easier to work with; those toward the tip are hard and brittle, and difficult to tie in without splitting.

9. Holding the quill sections together over the hook shank with the tips up, measure them so that the tips extend just beyond the bend of the hook. Using a soft loop (very critical with quill) tie the wing in just in front of the hackle. Your first wrap should be the farthest back. Take five to eight firm wraps forward and clip the excess quill.

10. Fill in the gap where the hook eye meets the shank. Use only enough turns of thread to build up a neatly tapered head. Finish with three half hitches or your whip finish tool. Trim the thread, cement the head, and clear the hook eye of cement with the excess hackle tip.

Introduction to Nymphs

Nymphs generally represent some form of aquatic insect in its nymphal, larval, or pupal stage. They are also tied to imitate crustaceans, such as scuds and cress bugs. It has been estimated that around 80% of a trout's diet consists of underwater organisms. Nymphs are tied to represent what fish eat most of the time.

Nymphs fall into two general categories: those that resemble a wide variety of food forms, and are referred to as *searching nymphs*, and those that are tied to represent a specific food form, called *imitative nymphs*.

Various nymphs are tied to fish anywhere from the surface film to thudding along the bottom. Some are therefore tied on light-wire hooks, with relatively buoyant materials, while others are tied on heavy hooks, with materials that absorb water fast. Nymphs are often weighted with lead wire, to get them down faster and to keep them on the bottom in turbulent currents.

Various Types of Nymph Flies

Traditional Nymph   Caddis Nymph   Mayfly Nymph

Steps in Tying a Typical Nymph

NYMPH PROPORTIONS:
Nymph proportions are not standardized because they are tied to represent such a wide variety of creatures.

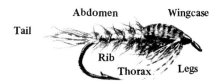

Tail   Abdomen   Wingcase   Rib   Thorax   Legs

GOLD RIBBED HARE'S EAR

Hook: Mustad 3906B, No. 6-16.
Thread: Black.
Weight: Ten-12 turns of lead wire, diameter of hook shank.
Tail: Tuft of hare's poll hair.
Rib: Medium gold tinsel.
Abdomen: Tan fur from hare's mask.
Wingcase: Brown mottled turkey.
Thorax: Darker fur from hare's mask, with guard hairs left in.

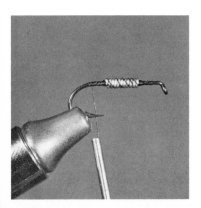

1. Place a size 8 hook in the vise. Lay base of thread wraps to hook bend. Wrap 10-12 turns of lead wire over the hook shank. The midpoint of the weight should be just forward of the midpoint of the hook. Spiral thread through lead, take a few wraps in front of lead, work thread to back of hook again, taking a few wraps behind lead.

2. Clip a small patch of fur from between the ears of a hare's mask. Leave most of the underfur in. Measure tail 1/2 the length of the hook shank, and tie it in at the bend of the hook. Clip three inches of medium tinsel and tie it in at the base of the tail. If you are using mylar, tie it in so the gold side is to the hook.

3. Clip a small patch of tan fur from the cheek area of a hare's mask. Remove the long guard hairs and work the dubbing into a two- or three-inch skein that is thin at one end and portly at the other. Wax your thread, hold the skein of fur against it, and twist it onto the thread. Wrap this to the midpoint of the hook shank.

4. Take three to five evenly-spaced wraps of tinsel over the abdomen fur. Take a few thread wraps around the tinsel, double it back over the wraps, and take a few more wraps over these. This locks the tinsel in. Trim the excess tinsel. Use medium tinsel on size 8 and 10 hooks; narrow tinsel on smaller hooks.

5. From a brown mottled turkey feather, clip a section about 1/4 to 3/8 inch wide. Lay this on top of the hook with the thinner, or tip, section toward the hook eye, the mottled side down. Tie it in, being sure that it is spread over the hook, not bunched up like the waist of a wasp. Tie it well back against the abdomen fur. Clip the excess.

6. Clip a small patch of darker fur from the hare's mask. Leave the guard hairs in and rough this into a short, loose skein. Wax the thread well, place the fur against it, and twist it *lightly* until it sticks. With the tip of your left index finger, form a loop of thread just longer than the dubbing. Fasten this down with a few wraps of thread.

7. Attach your hackle pliers or dubbing twister to the tip of the thread loop. Twirl them and watch the fur transform itself into a loose, spiky dubbing rope. This will not only give the fly life-like movement in the water, the guard hairs will also represent the legs of a natural insect. If the dubbing is tight after it is wrapped, pick it out with your bodkin.

8. Wrap this dubbing rope to the eye of the hook, being sure to start well back against the abdomen fur, forcing the turkey wingcase back over it so that it cannot leave a waist in the middle of the fly. Trim the excess dubbing rope. The thorax should be darker, slightly thicker, and not as neatly dubbed as the abdomen.

9. Pull the turkey wingcase forward, working it with your fingers so that it is spread out over the thorax. Tie it off with eight to ten firm wraps just behind the hook eye. Lift the portion sticking out over the front of the hook, and take the necessary turns to fill in the gap where the wire of the eye bends back and meets the hook shank.

10. Trim the excess of the wingcase, leaving a small portion in front of the hook eye. This looks like the head of an insect. Take a few wraps behind this, and tie off with half hitches or a whip finish there instead of at the eye of the hook. Clip the thread and cement the head well. On hook sizes 14 and smaller, the wingcase is often omitted on this fly.

Introduction to Steelhead and Salmon Flies

Although some dry flies are used to take summer steelhead and Atlantic salmon, for the most part they are taken on flies fished just below the surface. Winter steelhead and Pacific salmon take their flies right on the bottom.

A few steelhead flies, and quite a few Atlantic salmon patterns, get extremely complicated. They are dressed in exotic finery that would embarrass a dry, a wet, or a nymph. There is some debate whether all this beauty is built into the flies to please the fish or the fisherman. But beauty it is, and it is pleasant to fish with something so pleasing to the eye when it might be a long time between takes. Beauty lends confidence, and confidence helps catch fish.

Traditional Steelhead Fly   Low-water Salmon Fly   Traditional Atlantic Salmon Fly

Steps in Tying a Typical Steelhead Fly

SALMON & STEELHEAD FLY
PROPORTIONS:
Tail = shank length.
Hackle = shank length.
Wing = end of tail.

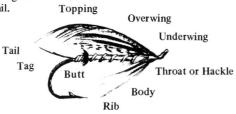

GREEN BUTT SKUNK

Hook: Mustad 36890, No. 4-10.
Thread: Black.
Wing: White calf tail.
Tail: Scarlet hackle fibers.
Butt: Green chenille.
Body: Black chenille.
Rib: Medium silver tinsel.
Hackle: Black.

1. Using the vise to hold it, de-barb and sharpen a size 6 hook. Place it in the vise for tying. Attach the thread just behind the fly eye. Lay a thread base over the front 1/5 of the hook shank. Cut a sparse clump of calf tail. The wing is tied in first to increase the durability of the fly. This is not true of more complicated salmon fly ties.

2. Holding the wing hair by the butts in your left thumb and forefinger, measure it the length of the hook. Move it forward and tie it in just behind the hook eye, with the butts toward the tail of the fly, the tips extending out over the eye. Wrap a tight layer of thread back over the wing butts and to the bend of the hook.

3. Select 15-20 fibers from a scarlet saddle hackle feather, extend them straight out from the stem, and pull them free. Measure them to a length equal to 2 hook gaps and tie them in so they extend straight out beyond the bend of the hook. Now lift them and take two wraps of thread under them to cock them upward. This will give the fly a rakish appearance.

4. Clip two inches of green chenille, and remove about 1/4 inch of fuzz from one end of it, exposing the threads. Tie this in at the base of the tail. Take two turns of the chenille, forming a butt, and tie it off. Clip the excess.

5. Clip four inches of black chenille, expose the threads, and tie it in just in front of the butt. Clip about four inches of tinsel, and tie this in just ahead of the body chenille. Wind your working thread to the wing. Wrap the black chenille to a point just behind the base of the wing and tie it off. Take the first turn of chenille behind the tinsel, the rest in front.

6. Wind four or five even turns of tinsel over the body. Tie the tinsel off, remembering to double it back over the first wraps, and taking a few extra wraps to hold it more securely. A well-tied salmon or steelhead fly should catch several fish. One poorly tied will end its first battle with its tinsel unwound, trailing like a pig's tail out behind it.

7. Select a hen or soft rooster hackle with fibers the length of the tail. Strip the fuzzy fibers from the base, and tie the feather in between the end of the body and the base of the wing. Be sure the concave side of the feather faces the hook shank. Clip excess stem.

8. Take three or four wraps of hackle, tie it off, and clip the excess tip. Work three or four turns of thread through the hackle, winding to the back and then back to the front, to hold it better. This will leave it looking disorganized, but you will police it up in a moment. Your hackle is just as likely as your tinsel to get cut by the teeth of a large fish.

9. With your left thumb, forefinger, and middle finger, draw the wing material back and hold it into the position it will have in the finished fly. Catch all of the stray hackle fibers along with the wing. Take a few thread wraps up over the wing base, to hold it in place, and to hold the hackle in the swept-back attitude you want.

10. Finish the fly with the number of wraps necessary to make a neatly tapered head. Tie it off with six half hitches or two whip finishes. Cement the head, and clear the hook eye. The wing, set on the hook in this manner, is tucked back beneath the body of the fly. It cannot work loose, no matter how fierce the steelhead or salmon you hook on the fly.

Streamers and Bucktails

The steps in tying streamers and bucktails are not unlike those in tying wet flies and steelhead or Atlantic salmon flies, except there are often more of them: streamers can be distressingly complex. The secret of making them easy is to use fine thread, tie each material carefully in the order in which it is listed in the dressing, and use no extra turns of thread. Then they are as simple to tie as any other fly.

The following section describes the steps in tying a Muddler Minnow, one of the most productive streamers, and one that requires a unique tying process that all tiers should learn because it can be used in so many different ways.

Introduction to Spun and Clipped Deer Hair

Spun deer hair has many uses, the most famous of which is the head of the Muddler, one of the best all around flies of all time. But it is also used in such trout flies as the Irresistible, and in many of the best bass bugs.

Because it is a unique process in fly tying, the method for spinning and clipping deer hair is covered here.

Spun and Clipped Deer Hair Flies

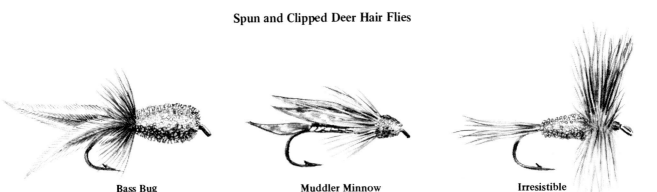

Bass Bug   Muddler Minnow   Irresistible

Steps in Tying a Muddler Head

1. On a No. 6 Mustad 9672 hook, tie a turkey quill tail. Wind a body of gold tinsel, starting 1/4 of the hook shank behind the head of the fly, winding the tinsel to the tail, then back again. Now tie an underwing of bucktail and an overwing of matched turkey quill sections, and you are ready to tie the head. Be sure you have left plenty of room for it.

2. From a piece of deer body hair clip a patch about half the diameter of a lead pencil. Work all of the fuzz out of the hair butts. If the tips are not even, align them with a hair stacker. Measure the hair so the tips extend approximately half the length of the wing, then clip the butts so they are about 1/2 inch longer than measured.

3. Holding the hair over the hook shank, take two soft loops around it. Let go of the hair at the same time you pull the loops tight. With your fingers, help the hair slip around the entire shank. Snug the hair down with several more wraps. Work the thread forward and take two or three wraps in front of the hair. Use your fingernails to pack the hair tightly back.

4. Clip a similar sized patch of hair from the skin. Clean out the fuzz. Clip both ends so the hair is 1/2 inch long. Using two soft loops pulled down slowly, spin this clump of hair in front of the other one. If additional hair is needed, pack this back and spin another batch. If not, tie off the fly head with several half hitches or your whip finish tool.

5. Holding the fly over a garbage can, use your scissors to clip the head to shape. First, use one blade of your scissors to depress the long collar fibers, clipping all around the back of the head. Then clip the bottom flat, leaving the collar sparse here. Next, clip the sides and top roughly to shape. Now clip the front into a neat taper. Finish with a final shaping.

Tying the Whip Finish

You will not want to finish flies with half hitches forever. A whip-finished head is stronger and neater. It is also one of the most elusive procedures in fly tying. Once you learn it, however, tying the whip finish is quick and easy. The right whip finish tool makes whip finishing easy. Learning without a tool is harder, but it saves time. The steps in tying a whip finish have been left to this last moment in the set of tying instructions because you've now developed some dexterity with your hands. Give it a try. Be patient.

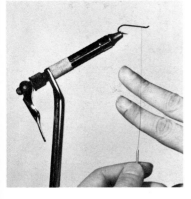

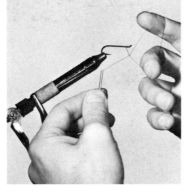

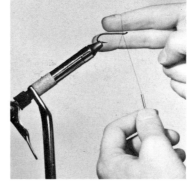

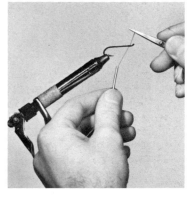

1. Affix thread to a bare hook. Spool 7-8 inches off the bobbin and grasp thread at bobbin tip with left thumb and forefinger. Extend your right forefinger and middle finger, *hold them so the back of your hand faces you,* then bring the fingers up *behind the thread.* The most common mistakes are to let the palm of your hand face you, and to place your fingers in front of the thread.

2. Roll your fingers toward you and to the right in a full circle, until the forefinger is on top, the fingers are looped by the thread, and the thread crosses to form an X between your fingers. The X is formed by the thread from the bobbin crossing *over* the thread from the hook.

3. Keep your fingers spread and force the X against the hook. Now drive your fingers straight back so the strands of the loop go one over and one under the hook. Let your fingers slide together and rotate them at the same time a half turn to the left, so the loop strands are reversed: the one that went under the hook is now on top, the one that went over is now under.

4. Bring your fingers down under the hook and up until the loop is in front of the hook. Now spread them again as in step 2. Repeat step 3 four times, for a whip finish of five turns. After the last loop, use your right thumb and forefinger tip (or your scissor's tip) to steer the loop into place while you pull it down tight with the bobbin.

Grizzly Saddle Patch

Blue Dun Cape

Brown Cape

Ginger Cape

Grizzly Cape

Blue Dun Hen Cape

Black Hen Cape

Golden Pheasant Cape

Calf Tail

Bucktail Patch

Squirrel Tail

Hare's Mask

Turkey Tails

Mallard Quills

Peacock Eye

Yellow, Green

& Black Marabou

Peacock Sword

Elk Hair

Light Deer Hair

Dark Deer Hair

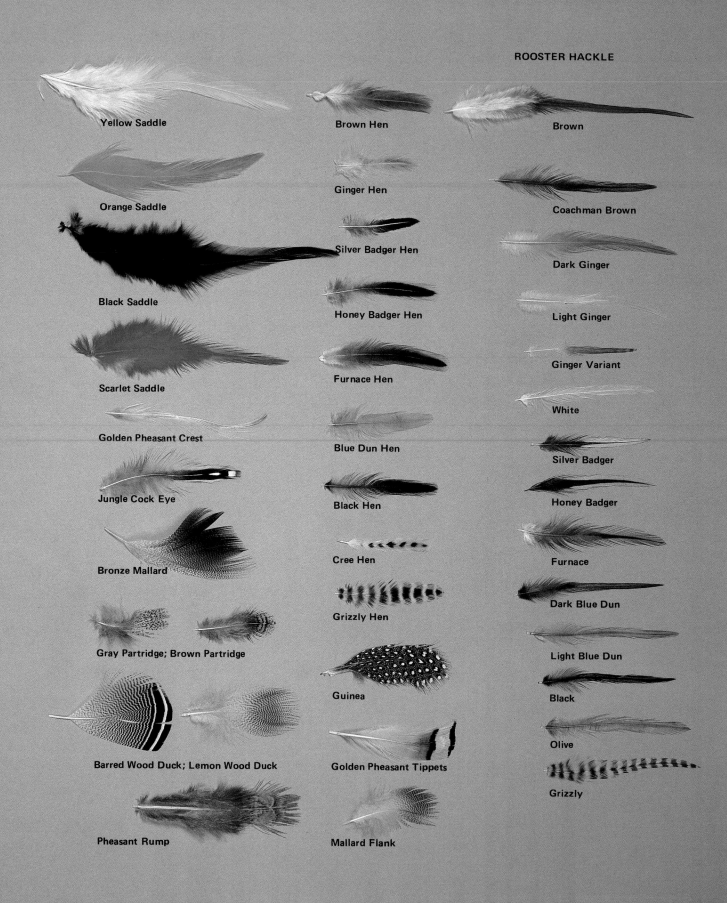

Yellow Saddle

Orange Saddle

Black Saddle

Scarlet Saddle

Golden Pheasant Crest

Jungle Cock Eye

Bronze Mallard

Gray Partridge; Brown Partridge

Barred Wood Duck; Lemon Wood Duck

Pheasant Rump

Brown Hen

Ginger Hen

Silver Badger Hen

Honey Badger Hen

Furnace Hen

Blue Dun Hen

Black Hen

Cree Hen

Grizzly Hen

Guinea

Golden Pheasant Tippets

Mallard Flank

Brown

Coachman Brown

Dark Ginger

Light Ginger

Ginger Variant

White

Silver Badger

Honey Badger

Furnace

Dark Blue Dun

Light Blue Dun

Black

Olive

Grizzly

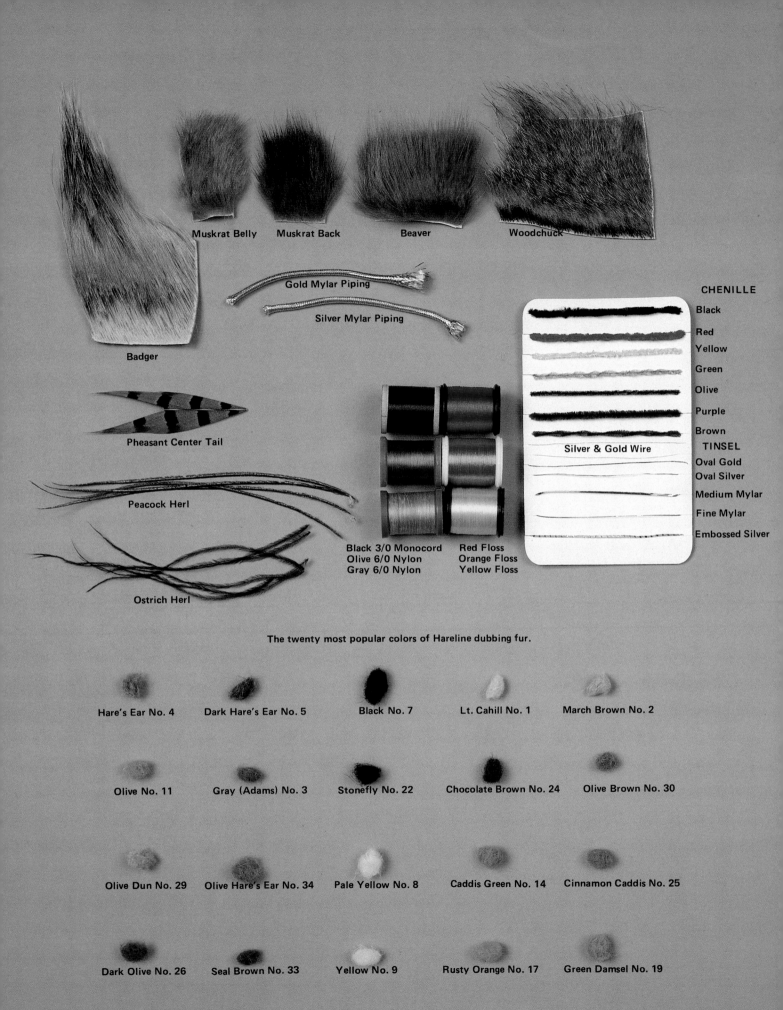

Muskrat Belly   Muskrat Back   Beaver   Woodchuck

Gold Mylar Piping

Silver Mylar Piping

Badger

CHENILLE

Black
Red
Yellow
Green
Olive
Purple
Brown

Pheasant Center Tail

Silver & Gold Wire

TINSEL

Oval Gold
Oval Silver
Medium Mylar
Fine Mylar
Embossed Silver

Peacock Herl

Ostrich Herl

Black 3/0 Monocord   Red Floss
Olive 6/0 Nylon   Orange Floss
Gray 6/0 Nylon   Yellow Floss

The twenty most popular colors of Hareline dubbing fur.

Hare's Ear No. 4   Dark Hare's Ear No. 5   Black No. 7   Lt. Cahill No. 1   March Brown No. 2

Olive No. 11   Gray (Adams) No. 3   Stonefly No. 22   Chocolate Brown No. 24   Olive Brown No. 30

Olive Dun No. 29   Olive Hare's Ear No. 34   Pale Yellow No. 8   Caddis Green No. 14   Cinnamon Caddis No. 25

Dark Olive No. 26   Seal Brown No. 33   Yellow No. 9   Rusty Orange No. 17   Green Damsel No. 19

Traditional Dry Flies

ADAMS
HOOK: *Mustad 94840, Nos. 10-20.*
THREAD: *Black.*
WING: *Grizzly hackle tips.*
TAIL: *Grizzly and brown hackle fibers, mixed.*
BODY: *Muskrat fur.*
HACKLE: *Grizzly and brown, mixed.*
NOTE: *Perhaps America's favorite dry fly, the Adams imitates a lot of things that trout eat. Grizzly hen hackle tips work well for the wings, and will save you lots of money if you tie lots of this dressing.*

BADGER SPIDER
HOOK: *Mustad 9523, Nos. 12-20.*
THREAD: *Black.*
TAIL: *Badger hackle fibers.*
HACKLE: *Badger, oversize.*
NOTE: *The Badger is just a sample Spider; they are also tied in black, blue dun, brown, furnace, ginger, and grizzly.*

BLACK GNAT
HOOK: *Mustad 94840, Nos. 12-20.*
THREAD: *Black.*
WINGS: *Mallard quill, upright and divided.*
TAIL: *Black hackle fibers.*
BODY: *Black dyed fur or synthetic.*
HACKLE: *Black.*
NOTE: *A popular variation has a red floss butt.*

BLUE QUILL
HOOK: *Mustad 94840, Nos. 10-18.*
THREAD: *Gray*
WINGS: *Blue dun hackle tips.*
TAIL: *Blue dun hackle fibers.*
RIB: *Silver wire, reverse wrapped.*
BODY: *Blue dun hackle stem.*
HACKLE: *Blue dun.*

BROWN BIVISIBLE
HOOK: *Mustad 94840, Nos. 10-16.*
THREAD: *Brown.*
BODY HACKLE: *Brown, three hackles wound length of body.*
FACE HACKLE: *White.*
NOTE: *Another listing for which there are many variations: badger, black, blue dun, furnace, ginger, grizzly, and olive, all with a white hackle at the front for visibility.*

Adams

Adams Parachute

Badger Spider

Badger Variant

Black Gnat

Blue Dun

Blue Quill

Blue Wing Olive

Brown Bivisible

Dark Cahill

ADAMS PARACHUTE
HOOK: *Mustad 94840, Nos. 6-18.*
THREAD: *Black.*
WING POST: *White calf tail.*
TAIL: *Moose body hair.*
BODY: *Muskrat fur.*
HACKLE: *Grizzly and brown, mixed, tied parachute.*
NOTE: *Parachute hackling is a style, and you can use that style on just about any dry fly, not just the Adams.*

BADGER VARIANT
HOOK: *Mustad 94840, Nos. 10-16.*
THREAD: *Black.*
WINGS: *Mallard quill, upright and divided.*
TAIL: *Badger hackle fibers.*
RIB: *Gray thread.*
BODY: *Black floss.*
HACKLE: *Badger.*
NOTE: *Again, the Badger is just a sample Variant; they are also tied in black, blue dun, brown, furnace, and ginger.*

BLUE DUN
HOOK: *Mustad 94840, Nos. 10-20.*
THREAD: *Black.*
WING: *Mallard quill, upright and divided.*
TAIL: *Blue dun hackle fibers.*
BODY: *Muskrat fur.*
HACKLE: *Blue dun.*
NOTE: *The Blue Dun and Blue Quill are examples of the traditional Catskill tie, based on the shape of the mayfly dun.*

BLUE WING OLIVE
HOOK: *Mustad 94840, Nos. 12-20.*
THREAD: *Olive.*
WING: *Dark blue dun hackle tips.*
TAIL: *Dark blue dun hackle fibers.*
BODY: *Brownish-olive fur.*
HACKLE: *Dark blue dun.*
NOTE: *This could have been listed as a mayfly dressing; it matches many species of mayflies with dun wings and olive bodies, in all areas of the country.*

DARK CAHILL
HOOK: *Mustad 94840, Nos. 10-20.*
THREAD: *Black.*
WINGS: *Wood duck flank, upright and divided.*
TAIL: *Brown hackle fibers.*
BODY: *Muskrat fur.*
HACKLE: *Brown.*
NOTE: *The Dark and Light Cahills, along with the Blue Dun or the Adams, combine to cover a color spectrum of mayfly species that hatch from coast to coast.*

LIGHT CAHILL

HOOK: *Mustad 94840, Nos. 10-20.*
THREAD: *Tan.*
WINGS: *Wood duck flank, upright and divided.*
TAIL: *Light ginger hackle fibers.*
BODY: *Cream badger underfur or synthetic.*
HACKLE: *Light ginger.*

GRAY FOX VARIANT

HOOK: *Mustad 94840, Nos. 10-12.*
THREAD: *Primrose silk.*
TAIL: *Ginger hackle fibers.*
BODY: *Light ginger hackle stem.*
HACKLE: *One light ginger, one dark ginger, one grizzly.*
NOTE: *One of the great Art Flick flies that doesn't look exactly like a natural insect but often cons trout better than an exact imitation.*

LIGHT HENDRICKSON

HOOK: *Mustad 94840, Nos. 10-16.*
THREAD: *Gray.*
WINGS: *Wood duck flank, upright and divided.*
TAIL: *Blue dun hackle fibers.*
BODY: *Light red fox fur.*
HACKLE: *Blue dun.*

PALE EVENING DUN

HOOK: *Mustad 94840, Nos. 12-16.*
THREAD: *White.*
WINGS: *Mallard quill, upright and divided.*
TIP: *Medium gold tinsel.*
TAIL: *White hackle fibers.*
BODY: *Cream fur or synthetic.*
HACKLE: *White.*

RED QUILL

HOOK: *Mustad 94840, Nos. 10-20.*
THREAD: *Yellow.*
WINGS: *Wood duck flank, upright and divided.*
TAIL: *Medium blue dun hackle fibers.*
BODY: *Dark brown hackle stem.*
HACKLE: *Medium blue dun.*
NOTE: *Soak the body hackle stem in water to reduce its brittleness and keep it from breaking when you wind it on the hook.*

Light Cahill

Ginger Quill

Gray Fox Variant

Dark Hendrickson

Light Hendrickson

March Brown

Pale Evening Dun

Quill Gordon

Red Quill

Royal Coachman

GINGER QUILL

HOOK: *Mustad 94840, Nos. 10-20.*
THREAD: *Tan.*
WINGS: *Mallard quill, upright and divided.*
TAIL: *Light ginger hackle fibers.*
RIB: *Gold wire, reverse wrapped.*
UNDERBODY: *Floss, any color, tapered.*
BODY: *Peacock quill.*
HACKLE: *Light ginger.*
NOTE: *The rib is reverse wrapped to protect the body from coming unravelled after catching trout.*

DARK HENDRICKSON

HOOK: *Mustad 94840, Nos. 10-16.*
THREAD: *Gray.*
WINGS: *Wood duck flank, upright and divided.*
TAIL: *Dark blue dun hackle fibers.*
BODY: *Muskrat fur.*
HACKLE: *Dark blue dun.*
NOTE: *The Dark and Light Hendricksons are two more Catskill ties that match a variety of mayflies, far beyond the waters where they were created.*

MARCH BROWN

HOOK: *Mustad 94840, Nos. 10-16.*
THREAD: *Orange.*
WING: *Wood duck flank, upright and divided.*
TAIL: *Ginger hackle fibers.*
BODY: *Light red fox fur.*
HACKLE: *Dark ginger and grizzly, mixed.*

QUILL GORDON

HOOK: *Mustad 94840, Nos. 10-20.*
THREAD: *Pale yellow.*
WINGS: *Wood duck flank, upright and divided.*
TAIL: *Rusty blue dun hackle fibers.*
BODY: *Stripped white/dark peacock quill.*
HACKLE: *Rusty blue dun.*
NOTE: *The most famous fly of Theodore Gordon, who has been called the father of American dry fly fishing.*

ROYAL COACHMAN

HOOK: *Mustad, Nos. 10-20.*
THREAD: *Black.*
WINGS: *White mallard quill, upright and divided.*
TAIL: *Golden pheasant tippet.*
BODY: *Peacock herl/red floss/peacock herl.*
HACKLE: *Coachman brown.*
NOTE: *Right up there with the Adams for popularity. It doesn't look like any insect, but it is visible to the angler, and it must look like something good to eat to a trout, because it still catches a lot of them.*

Hairwing Dry Flies

AUSABLE WULFF
HOOK: *Mustad 7957B, Nos. 6-16.*
THREAD: *Fluorescent red.*
WING: *White calf tail, upright and divided.*
TAIL: *Woodchuck tail fibers.*
BODY: *Rusty orange Aussie opossum fir.*
HACKLE: *Mixed brown and grizzly.*
NOTE: *The high-floating Wulff series drys, originated by Lee Wulff, are among the best for fast water, and are also used to entice Atlantic salmon up to the surface.*

GRIZZLY WULFF
HOOK: *Mustad 7957B, Nos. 6-16.*
THREAD: *Black.*
WINGS: *Brown bucktail.*
TAIL: *Brown bucktail.*
BODY: *Yellow floss or fur.*
HACKLE: *Brown and grizzly, mixed.*
NOTE: *This buggy dressing, with its yellow body and variegated hackle, is a good one whenever terrestrial insects are getting into trouble with trout.*

HOUSE AND LOT VARIANT
HOOK: *Mustad 94840, Nos. 10-16.*
THREAD: *Black.*
WINGS: *White calf tail.*
TAIL: *White calf tail.*
RIB: *Gold wire, reverse wrapped.*
BODY: *Rear half dark peacock quill. Front half peacock herl.*
HACKLE: *Furnace.*
NOTE: *It doesn't look like any may- fly you will ever see, but toss this one out during a hatch of any large mayfly species and the results will surprise you, even over selective trout.*

ROYAL HUMPY
HOOK: *Mustad 7957B, Nos. 6-16.*
THREAD: *Red.*
TAIL: *Dark moose hair.*
UNDERBODY: *Red thread wound over butts of overbody deer hair.*
OVERBODY: *Deer hair pulled forward to make shellback.*
WINGS: *White calf tail, upright and divided.*
HACKLE: *Brown.*

IRRESISTIBLE
HOOK: *Mustad 7957B, Nos. 6-16.*
THREAD: *Black.*
TAIL: *Brown bucktail.*
BODY: *Deer body hair, spun and clipped.*
WING: *Brown bucktail.*
HACKLE: *Medium or dark blue dun.*
NOTE: *An irresistibly buggy looking fly.*

GRAY WULFF
HOOK: *Mustad 7957B, Nos. 6-16.*
THREAD: *Black.*
WING: *Brown bucktail.*
TAIL: *Brown bucktail.*
BODY: *Muskrat fur.*
HACKLE: *Medium or dark blue dun.*

ROYAL WULFF
HOOK: *Mustad 7957B, Nos. 6-16.*
THREAD: *Black.*
WING: *White calf tail.*
TAIL: *White calf tail.*
BODY: *Peacock herl/red floss/peacock herl.*
HACKLE: *Coachman brown.*
NOTE: *There are few patterns that offer a higher float, better visibility to the fisherman, and more attraction to the trout than this one. It's a number one searching dry fly for fast water.*

HUMPY
HOOK: *Mustad 7957B, Nos. 6-16.*
THREAD: *Yellow.*
TAIL: *Deer body hair.*
UNDERBODY: *Yellow thread over butts of body and wing deer hair.*
OVERBODY: *Same deer hair pulled forward over underbody.*
WING: *Same deer hair tips tied upright and divided.*
HACKLE: *Grizzly and brown, mixed.*
NOTE: *An easy one to tie once you get the hang of it. And there is no fly that catches more trout in a wider variety of circumstances. A special favorite in the Rocky Mountain states.*

ROYAL TRUDE
HOOK: *Mustad 7957B, Nos. 6-16.*
THREAD: *Black.*
TAIL: *Golden pheasant tippets.*
RIB: *Gold wire, reverse wrapped.*
BODY: *Peacock herl/red floss/ peacock herl.*
WING: *White calf tail.*
HACKLE: *Coachman brown.*

COLORADO KING
HOOK: *Mustad 94840, Nos. 6-16.*
THREAD: *Brown.*
TAILS: *Peccary or moose.*
HACKLE: *Brown, palmered.*
BODY: *Hare's mask fur.*
WING: *Deer body hair.*
NOTE: *This dressing can also be tied with a muskrat or a yellow fur body and grizzly hackle. It gives an excellent caddisfly, stonefly, or grasshopper silhouette on the water.*

Ausable Wulff

Gray Wulff

Grizzly Wulff

Royal Wulff

House and Lot Variant

Humpy

Royal Humpy

Royal Trude

Irresistible

Colorado King

Mayfly Dry Flies

BLUE UPRIGHT

HOOK: *Mustad 94840, Nos. 12-20.*
THREAD: *Gray.*
WINGS: *Mallard quill, upright and divided.*
TAIL: *Blue dun hackle fibers.*
RIB: *Silver wire, reverse wrapped.*
BODY: *Peacock quill.*
HACKLE: *Blue dun.*
NOTE: *Does a fine job of imitating most gray-bodied mayfly duns. The Blue Upright and Blue Quill are similar patterns that also imitate grayish mayfly duns.*

GREEN DRAKE

HOOK: *Mustad 94840, Nos. 10-14.*
THREAD: *Olive.*
WINGS: *Natural dun deer hair, upright and divided.*
TAIL: *Natural dun deer hair.*
BODY: *Olive fur.*
HACKLE: *Grizzly and brown, mixed.*
NOTE: *This is a rough-water imitation based on the Wulff series of flies.*

THORAX HENDRICKSON

HOOK: *Mustad 94833, Nos. 14-16.*
THREAD: *Gray.*
TAILS: *Blue dun hackle fibers, split.*
BODY: *Muskrat fur.*
WING: *Blue dun hen hackle fibers.*
HACKLE: *Blue dun.*
NOTE: *The Thorax ties offer a slightly more true silhouette of the natural mayfly dun, when compared to the traditional Catskill ties. Any traditional dressing can be tied in the Thorax style.*

MARCH BROWN COMPARA-DUN

HOOK: *Mustad 94833, Nos. 12-16.*
THREAD: *Tan.*
WING: *Tan deer leg hair, flared 180 degrees over hook.*
TAILS: *Nutria or beaver guard hair fibers, split.*
BODY: *Tan hare's ear fur or synthetic.*
NOTE: *Tie the wing in first on this one, then the rest of the fly around it. Can be varied to meet any mayfly hatch. Is an excellent style where imitation is important, but flotation is also needed.*

SULPHUR CUT-WING DUN

HOOK: *Mustad 94833, Nos. 12-18.*
THREAD: *Yellow.*
TAILS: *Light ginger hackle fibers, split.*
WINGS: *Light ginger hen hackle tips, cut to shape.*
BODY: *Pale yellow fur or synthetic.*
HACKLE: *Light ginger, tied parachute.*
NOTE: *For the patient tier, this style makes about as close a copy of the natural as you will find.*

Blue Upright

Blue-Wing Olive No-hackle

Green Drake

Hen Spinner

Thorax Hendrickson

Little Olive Parachute

March Brown Compara-dun

Cream Compara-spinner

Sulphur Cut-wing Dun

Trico Poly-wing Spinner

BLUE-WING OLIVE NO-HACKLE

HOOK: *Mustad 94833, Nos. 14-24.*
THREAD: *Olive.*
TAILS: *Blue dun hackles fibers, split.*
BODY: *Olive fur.*
WINGS: *Teal quill sections.*
NOTE: *The no-hackle flies, popularized by Swisher and Richards in* Selective Trout, *can be tied in sizes and colors to imitate any mayfly hatch. They are excellent where fish are critical and flotation is not.*

HEN SPINNER

HOOK: *Mustad 94833, Nos. 12-20.*
THREAD: *Brown.*
TAIL: *Blue dun hackle fibers, split.*
BODY: *Reddish-brown fur or synthetic.*
WINGS: *Blue dun hen hackle tips.*
NOTE: *This general concept can be used to imitate any mayfly female spent and lying on the water. A hackle can be wound round the wings and clipped top and bottom for better flotation.*

LITTLE OLIVE PARACHUTE

HOOK: *Mustad 94833, Nos. 16-22.*
THREAD: *Olive.*
WING POST: *White calf body hair.*
TAILS: *Blue dun hackle fibers, split.*
BODY: *Olive fur.*
HACKLE: *Blue dun, tied parachute.*
NOTE: *The parachute style has the advantage of lowering the body of the fly right down into the water, offering a very natural outline of the natural mayfly.*

CREAM COMPARA-SPINNER

HOOK: *Mustad 94833, Nos. 12-18.*
THREAD: *White.*
TAILS: *Light ginger hackle fibers, split.*
BODY: *Cream fur or synthetic.*
WINGS: *Light ginger hackle, clipped top and bottom.*
NOTE: *An excellent spinner pattern, and one that will be useful in variations of color and size, for all mayfly spinner falls.*

TRICO POLY-WING SPINNER

HOOK: *Mustad 94833, Nos. 20-26.*
THREAD: *White.*
TAILS: *White hackle fibers, split.*
ABDOMEN: *Olive fur or synthetic.*
WINGS: *Polypro yarn, tied spent.*
THORAX: *Brown fur or synthetic.*
NOTE: *The flies listed on this page are all samples of pattern styles that can be varied in size and color to match the dun and spinner stages of many mayfly species on various water types.*

Stonefly Dry Flies

BIRD'S STONE FLY

HOOK: *Mustad 9672, Nos. 4-8.*
THREAD: *Orange.*
TAIL: *Two strands moose hair.*
RIB: *Trimmed furnace saddle hackle.*
BODY: *Orange floss.*
WING: *Bucktail.*
HACKLE: *Furnace.*
ANTENNAE: *Two strands moose hair.*
NOTE: *Substitute stripped brown hackle stems for the moose hair on the tails and antennae of this one if it looks better to you.*

GOLDEN STONE

HOOK: *Mustad 38941, Nos. 6-8.*
THREAD: *Gold.*
RIB: *Dyed gold hackle, palmered.*
BODY: *Gold synthetic yarn.*
WING: *Bucktail dyed gold.*
HACKLE: *Dyed gold saddle.*

LITTLE YELLOW STONE

HOOK: *Mustad 38941, Nos. 10-12.*
THREAD: *Yellow.*
TAIL: *Grizzly hackle fibers dyed pale yellow.*
REAR HACKLE: *Grizzly dyed pale yellow.*
RIB: *Yellow thread.*
BODY: *Chartreuse synthetic yarn.*
FRONT HACKLE: *Grizzly dyed pale yellow.*

IMPROVED SOFA PILLOW

HOOK: *Mustad 9672, Nos. 4-10.*
THREAD: *Brown.*
TAIL: *Orange dyed elk hair.*
RIB: *Brown hackle, palmered.*
BODY: *Orange fur or synthetic.*
WING: *Woodchuck tail.*
HACKLE: *Brown.*
NOTE: *This improved version works much better than the original when the salmon fly is on the water.*

TROTH SALMON FLY

HOOK: *Mustad 79580, Nos. 4-8.*
THREAD: *Brown.*
TAIL: *Brown elk hair.*
RIB: *Orange thread.*
BODY: *Orange bucktail.*
UNDERWING: *Brown elk hair.*
OVERWING: *Fluorescent orange bucktail.*
HEAD AND HACKLE: *Brown elk hair.*
NOTE: *These Al Troth dressings for the salmon fly and golden stone fly (following) are excellent in silhouette. They float flush in the water, and entice up the largest trout.*

Bird's Stone Fly

Dark Stone

Golden Stone

Little Brown Stone

Little Yellow Stone

Sofa Pillow

Improved Sofa Pillow

Stimulator

Troth Salmon Fly

Yellow Stone Fly

DARK STONE

HOOK: *Mustad 38941, Nos. 6-8.*
THREAD: *Black.*
RIB: *Furnace hackle, palmered.*
BODY: *Orange synthetic yarn.*
WING: *Brown bucktail.*
HACKLE: *Dark furnace.*
NOTE: *The Dark Stone and the Golden Stone are patterns from the famous Oregon tier, Polly Rosborough.*

LITTLE BROWN STONE

HOOK: *Mustad 38941, Nos. 12-14.*
THREAD: *Brown.*
TAIL: *Ringneck pheasant body fibers.*
RIB: *Brown thread.*
BODY: *Seal brown synthetic yarn.*
WING: *Single grizzly hackle tip.*
HACKLE: *Grizzly.*
NOTE: *Rick Hafele, co-author of Western Hatches and instructor in the Scientific Anglers tape, Anatomy of a Trout Stream, ties a similar pattern with a woodchuck hair wing.*

SOFA PILLOW

HOOK: *Mustad 9672, Nos. 4-10.*
THREAD: *Black.*
TAIL: *Crimson goose quill section.*
BODY: *Red floss.*
WING: *Red fox squirrel tail.*
HACKLE: *Brown.*
NOTE: *One of the oldest dressings around for the stoneflies. Works for both the salmon fly and the golden stone.*

STIMULATOR

HOOK: *Mustad 9672, Nos. 6-16.*
THREAD: *Orange.*
TAIL: *Deer body hair.*
RIB: *Grizzly hackle, palmered.*
ABDOMEN: *Yellow fur.*
WING: *Deer body hair.*
HACKLE: *Grizzly, palmered through thorax.*
THORAX: *Orange fur.*
NOTE: *The Stimulator is an excellent dressing when smaller yellow-bodied stoneflies are out. It is also a good searching pattern, reminiscent to trout of the many caddisflies and grasshoppers they have eaten over the years.*

YELLOW STONE FLY

HOOK: *Mustad 79580, Nos. 6-10.*
THREAD: *Brown.*
TAIL: *Brown elk body hair.*
RIB: *Yellow thread.*
BODY: *Yellow dyed bucktail.*
UNDERWING: *Brown elk hair.*
OVERWING: *Fluorescent yellow bucktail.*
HEAD AND HACKLE: *Brown elk hair.*

Caddis Dry Flies

DARK CADDIS

HOOK: *Mustad 7957B, Nos. 8-14.*
THREAD: *Yellow.*
TAIL: *Yellow hackle fibers.*
HACKLE: *Yellow, palmered.*
BODY: *Yellow fur or synthetic.*
WING: *Dark deer body hair.*
NOTE: *This dressing floats well and fishes for most of the dark colored species of caddisflies.*

TAN ELK HAIR CADDIS

HOOK: *Mustad 94840, Nos. 10-20.*
THREAD: *Tan.*
RIB: *Gold wire, wound over body and hackle.*
BODY: *Hare's ear fur.*
HACKLE: *Furnace.*
WING: *Tan elk hair.*
NOTE: *This Al Troth dressing might be the number one dry fly in the West now. It gives the silhouette of the natural, floats like a cork, and is visible even on a long cast into rough water.*

DEER HAIR CADDIS

HOOK: *Mustad 94840, Nos. 10-20.*
THREAD: *Gray.*
BODY: *Olive fur or synthetic.*
HACKLE: *Blue dun.*
WING: *Natural dun deer hair.*
NOTE: *This dressing, popularized by noted fishing photographer Jim Schollmeyer, is an Elk Hair Caddis-type dressing that imitates the numerous dun colored species of caddisflies.*

HENRYVILLE SPECIAL

HOOK: *Mustad 94840, Nos. 14-20.*
THREAD: *Brown.*
RIB: *Grizzly hackle.*
BODY: *Olive fur.*
UNDERWING: *Wood duck flank.*
OVERWING: *Mallard quill.*
HACKLE: *Dark ginger.*

QUILL-WING CADDIS

HOOK: *Mustad 94833, Nos. 10-16.*
THREAD: *Gray.*
BODY: *Light olive fur.*
WING: *Turkey quill.*
HACKLE: *Dark ginger.*
NOTE: *The Quill-wing Caddis can be varied in color and size to meet any of the caddis hatches. It is excellent in still- and slow-water situations.*

Dark Caddis

Light Caddis

Tan Elk Hair Caddis

Brown Elk Hair Caddis

Deer Hair Caddis

Fluttering Caddis

Henryville Special

Kings River Caddis

Quill-wing Caddis

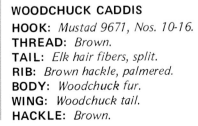

Woodchuck Caddis

LIGHT CADDIS

HOOK: *Mustad 7957B, Nos. 8-14.*
THREAD: *Tan.*
TAIL: *Tan elk hair.*
HACKLE: *Light ginger, palmered.*
BODY: *Light yellow fur or synthetic.*
WING: *Tan elk body hair.*
NOTE: *Paired with the Dark Caddis above, this dressing covers a lot of the spectrum of caddis colors.*

BROWN ELK HAIR CADDIS

HOOK: *Mustad 94840, Nos. 10-20.*
THREAD: *Brown.*
RIB: *Gold wire.*
BODY: *Olive fur or synthetic.*
HACKLE: *Brown, palmered.*
WING: *Brown dyed elk hair.*
NOTE: *A variation on the standard Elk Hair Caddis, this one combines with the tan color to cover the colors of most caddis species.*

FLUTTERING CADDIS

HOOK: *Mustad 94840, Nos. 10-18.*
THREAD: *Black.*
BODY: *Olive-brown fur or synthetic.*
WING: *Gray minktail guard fibers.*
HACKLE: *Dark blue dun.*
NOTE: *The Fluttering Caddis is designed to be moved on the water, fished like the living insect.*

KINGS RIVER CADDIS

HOOK: *Mustad 94840, Nos. 10-16.*
THREAD: *Brown.*
BODY: *Raccoon fur.*
WINGS: *Mottled brown turkey quill.*
HACKLE: *Brown.*

WOODCHUCK CADDIS

HOOK: *Mustad 9671, Nos. 10-16.*
THREAD: *Brown.*
TAIL: *Elk hair fibers, split.*
RIB: *Brown hackle, palmered.*
BODY: *Woodchuck fur.*
WING: *Woodchuck tail.*
HACKLE: *Brown.*

Midge Dry Flies

ADAMS MIDGE

HOOK: *Mustad 94842, Nos. 16-26.*
THREAD: *Black.*
TAIL: *Grizzly hackle fibers.*
BODY: *Muskrat fur.*
HACKLE: *Grizzly.*
NOTE: *This one can also be tied with tail and hackle of brown and grizzly mixed, as it is called for in the traditional Adams.*

BLACK MIDGE

HOOK: *Mustad 94842, Nos. 16-26.*
THREAD: *Black.*
TAIL: *Black hackle fibers.*
BODY: *Black thread.*
HACKLE: *Black.*

DUN MIDGE

HOOK: *Mustad 94842, Nos. 16-26.*
THREAD: *Gray.*
TAILS: *Blue dun hackle fibers.*
BODY: *Muskrat fur.*
HACKLE: *Blue dun.*
NOTE: *Effective when very small grayish mayflies are on the water; also when the general run of midges are about.*

GRAY HERL MIDGE

HOOK: *Mustad 94833, Nos. 20-28.*
THREAD: *Gray.*
TAILS: *Blue dun hackle fibers.*
BODY: *Gray ostrich herl.*

LITTLE OLIVE

HOOK: *Mustad 94833, Nos. 18-22.*
THREAD: *Olive.*
TAIL: *Blue dun hackle fibers.*
BODY: *Tannish-olive fur.*
WINGS: *Blue dun hackle tips.*
HACKLE: *Blue dun.*
NOTE: *This fly was originated by Ed Koch specifically for the Little Olive mayflies, of the Baetis genus, that hatch on his Pennsylvania waters. It works well across the country.*

Adams Midge

Badger Midge

Black Midge

Cream Midge

Dun Midge

Black Herl Midge

Gray Herl Midge

Griffith's Gnat

Little Olive

Mosquito

BADGER MIDGE

HOOK: *Mustad 94842, Nos. 16-26.*
THREAD: *Black.*
TAIL: *Badger hackle fibers.*
BODY: *Stripped peacock quill.*
HACKLE: *Badger.*
NOTE: *All of the midge dressings are designed to be fished whenever trout are taking any small insects, whether they be mayflies, or the true midges, members of the family Chironomidae.*

CREAM MIDGE

HOOK: *Mustad 94842, Nos. 16-26.*
THREAD: *White.*
TAIL: *Cream hackle fibers.*
BODY: *Cream fur.*
HACKLE: *Cream.*
NOTE: *This one is especially effective during hatches of tiny cream-colored mayflies.*

BLACK HERL MIDGE

HOOK: *Mustad 94833, Nos. 20-28.*
THREAD: *Black.*
TAIL: *Black hackle fibers.*
BODY: *Black ostrich herl.*
NOTE: *Designed to be fished in the surface film, it gives the impression of the insect in, not on, the water.*

GRIFFITH'S GNAT

HOOK: *Mustad 94842, Nos. 18-28.*
THREAD: *Olive.*
HACKLE: *Grizzly, palmered.*
BODY: *Peacock herl.*
NOTE: *When tied with a good grade of grizzly hackle, this one looks like a fat little Woolly Worm, but fishes the surface film. Try it during any midge hatch when you can't catch fish. It will surprise you. Pleasantly.*

MOSQUITO

HOOK: *Mustad 94840, Nos. 12-18.*
THREAD: *Black.*
WINGS: *Grizzly hackle tips, upright and divided.*
TAIL: *Grizzly hackle fibers.*
BODY: *Dark and light moose mane fibers, together.*
HACKLE: *Grizzly.*
NOTE: *Mosquitoes are used most in high mountain lakes.*

Terrestrials

Black Ant

Cinnamon Ant

Flying Black Ant

Black Beetle

Black Feather Beetle

Jassid

Green Inch Worm

Joe's Hopper

Letort Hopper

Letort Cricket

BLACK ANT

HOOK: *Mustad 94840, Nos. 14-22.*
THREAD: *Black.*
ABDOMEN: *Black fur or synthetic.*
HACKLE: *Black, two or three turns.*
THORAX: *Black fur or synthetic.*
NOTE: *This dressing can be treated with floatant and fished in the surface film, or it can be left untreated and fished under the surface, as a wet fly.*

FLYING BLACK ANT

HOOK: *Mustad 94840, Nos. 12-18.*
THREAD: *Black.*
ABDOMEN: *Black fur or synthetic.*
WINGS: *Blue dun hackle tips.*
HACKLE: *Black, two or three turns.*
THORAX: *Black fur or synthetic.*
NOTE: *Again, this can be fished as either a dry or wet fly, depending on how you treat it and how you fish it.*

BLACK FEATHER BEETLE

HOOK: *Mustad 94833, Nos. 12-20.*
THREAD: *Black.*
BODY: *Peacock herl.*
HACKLE: *Black, palmered, trimmed top and bottom.*
WING: *Two feathers from ringneck pheasant collar, trimmed to shape.*

GREEN INCH WORM

HOOK: *Mustad 94833, Nos. 10-14.*
THREAD: *Green.*
BODY: *Yellowish-green bucktail, segmented with thread.*

LETORT HOPPER

HOOK: *Mustad 9671, Nos. 10-14.*
THREAD: *Yellow.*
BODY: *Yellow fur or synthetic.*
UNDERWING: *Mottled turkey quill.*
OVERWING: *Deer body hair.*
HEAD: *Spun and clipped butts of overwing.*
NOTE: *This is one of the easier hopper patterns to tie, and also one of the most effective, and not just on Pennsylvania's famous Letort Spring Creek.*

CINNAMON ANT

HOOK: *Mustad 94840, Nos. 14-22.*
THREAD: *Brown.*
ABDOMEN: *Brown fur or synthetic.*
HACKLE: *Brown.*
THORAX: *Brown fur or synthetic.*
NOTE: *The brown and black ants are by far most common, and are much more common in trout diets than most anglers notice.*

BLACK BEETLE

HOOK: *Mustad 94840, Nos. 10-20.*
THREAD: *Black.*
SHELLBACK: *Black deer body hair or black goose quill.*
HACKLE: *Black, palmered and trimmed.*
BODY: *Black fur or synthetic.*
NOTE: *Beetles, especially in the smaller sizes, are often what fish are taking when we can see that they are taking something but can't, no matter how hard we try, see exactly what it is.*

JASSID

HOOK: *Mustad 94840, Nos. 16-22.*
THREAD: *Black.*
BODY: *Black hackle, palmered, clipped top and bottom.*
WING: *Jungle cock eye or substitute.*

JOE'S HOPPER

HOOK: *Mustad 94831, Nos. 6-12.*
THREAD: *Brown.*
TAIL: *Scarlet hackle fibers.*
RIB: *Brown hackle, trimmed to reverse taper.*
BODY: *Light yellow polypro yarn; extend over tail.*
WING: *Turkey quill.*
HACKLE: *Brown and grizzly, mixed.*

LETORT CRICKET

HOOK: *Mustad 9671, Nos. 10-14.*
THREAD: *Black.*
BODY: *Black fur or synthetic.*
UNDERWING: *Black goose quill.*
OVERWING: *Black deer body hair.*
HEAD: *Spun and clipped butts of overwing.*

Traditional Wet Flies

ALDER
HOOK: *Mustad 3906, Nos. 10-14.*
THREAD: *Black.*
BODY: *Peacock herl.*
HACKLE: *Black hen.*
WING: *Mottled turkey quill.*
NOTE: *Based on an old traditional British pattern, the Alder matches the alderfly here as well as it does there. It's effective from coast to coast.*

BLUE QUILL
HOOK: *Mustad 3906, Nos. 12-18.*
THREAD: *White.*
TAILS: *Blue dun hackle fibers.*
BODY: *Bleached peacock quill.*
HACKLE: *Pale blue dun hen hackle.*
WING: *Mallard quill.*
NOTE: *Sparse wet flies fished just under the surface can be more effective than dry flies during mayfly spinner falls. This is a good one when grayish mayflies are falling.*

LIGHT CAHILL
HOOK: *Mustad 3906, Nos. 8-16.*
THREAD: *Cream.*
TAIL: *Wood duck flank.*
BODY: *Cream fox fur.*
HACKLE: *Light ginger.*
WING: *Wood duck flank.*
NOTE: *Try this wet fly when cream-colored mayflies are hatching and you aren't doing much on dry flies. Fish might be taking the ascending nymphs.*

LEADWING COACHMAN
HOOK: *Mustad 3906, Nos. 10-16.*
THREAD: *Black.*
TAG: *Medium gold tinsel.*
BODY: *Peacock herl.*
HACKLE: *Coachman brown.*
WING: *Mallard quill.*
NOTE: *This is a variation of the Coachman and is truer to the natural colors of insects. The herl body reflects tiny points of light and gives the fly a life-like look.*

GINGER QUILL
HOOK: *Mustad 3906, Nos. 12-18.*
THREAD: *White.*
TAILS: *Wood duck flank.*
BODY: *Ginger hackle stem.*
HACKLE: *Pale ginger hen.*
WINGS: *Mallard quill.*
NOTE: *This can be a deadly pattern during emergences and spinner falls of pale-colored mayflies.*

Alder

Black Gnat

Blue Quill

Dark Cahill

Light Cahill

Coachman

Leadwing Coachman

Royal Coachman

Ginger Quill

Gray Hackle Peacock

BLACK GNAT
HOOK: *Mustad 3906, Nos. 8-16.*
THREAD: *Black.*
BODY: *Black chenille.*
HACKLE: *Black hen.*
WING: *Goose or mallard quill.*

DARK CAHILL
HOOK: *Mustad 3906, Nos. 8-16.*
THREAD: *Black.*
TAIL: *Wood duck flank.*
BODY: *Muskrat fur.*
HACKLE: *Brown.*
WING: *Wood duck flank.*
NOTE: *Just as in the dry flies, the Dark and Light Cahill wets cover a wide color spectrum of natural trout foods, and are also terrors on bluegills.*

COACHMAN
HOOK: *Mustad 3906, Nos. 10-16.*
THREAD: *Black.*
TAG: *Medium gold tinsel.*
BODY: *Peacock herl.*
HACKLE: *Coachman brown hen.*
WING: *White mallard quill.*
NOTE: *Tie this one with the herl rope, twisted on your thread, that was mentioned in the introductory chapters. Herl that is simply wound on will be cut by the teeth of the first fish.*

ROYAL COACHMAN
HOOK: *Mustad 3906, Nos. 10-16.*
THREAD: *Black.*
TAIL: *Golden pheasant tippets.*
BODY: *Peacock herl/red floss/ peacock herl.*
HACKLE: *Coachman brown.*
WING: *White mallard quill.*
NOTE: *Like the Royal Coachman dry, this fly doesn't look like any insect, but it accounts for a lot of caught trout. And its colors make it a natural for panfish, too.*

GRAY HACKLE PEACOCK
HOOK: *Mustad 3906, Nos. 10-16.*
THREAD: *Black.*
TAG: *Medium gold tinsel.*
TAIL: *Scarlet hackle fibers.*
BODY: *Peacock herl.*
HACKLE: *Grizzly hen.*
NOTE: *The red, peacock, and grizzly make this a killing combination.*

HARE'S EAR

HOOK: *Mustad 3906, Nos. 8-16.*
THREAD: *Black.*
TAIL: *Brown hackle fibers.*
RIB: *Medium gold tinsel.*
BODY: *Hare's ear fur, with guard hairs left in.*
WING: *Mallard quill.*
NOTE: *The rabbit fur guard hairs serve as the hackle on this one.*

LIGHT HENDRICKSON

HOOK: *Mustad 3906, Nos. 10-16.*
THREAD: *Gray.*
TAIL: *Pale blue dun hackle fibers.*
BODY: *Light red fox fur.*
HACKLE: *Pale blue dun.*
WING: *Wood duck flank.*

McGINTY

HOOK: *Mustad 3906, Nos. 8-12.*
THREAD: *Black.*
TAIL: *Scarlet hackle fibers under, teal flank over.*
BODY: *Yellow chenille/black chenille/ yellow chenille.*
HACKLE: *Brown hen.*
WINGS: *White-tipped mallard secondary.*
NOTE: *Of course this one imitates the drowned bumblebee.*

PICKET PIN

HOOK: *Mustad 9671, Nos. 8-12.*
THREAD: *Black.*
TAIL: *Brown hackle fibers.*
RIB: *Brown hackle, palmered.*
BODY: *Peacock herl.*
WING: *White-tipped squirrel tail.*
HEAD: *Peacock herl.*
NOTE: *Another fly that looks like nothing but catches fish well. Peacock herl seems to fool fish no matter how it is used.*

BLACK WOOLLY WORM

HOOK: *Mustad 9671, Nos. 2-14.*
THREAD: *Black.*
TAIL: *Scarlet hackle fibers.*
HACKLE: *Grizzly, palmered.*
BODY: *Black chenille.*
NOTE: *The Black and Brown Woolly Worms listed are just the tip of an iceberg. Woolly Worms are tied in simply every combination of body and hackle color that you can imagine.*

Hare's Ear

Dark Hendrickson

Light Hendrickson

Hornberg

McGinty

March Brown

Picket Pin

Quill Gordon

Black Woolly Worm

Brown Woolly Worm

DARK HENDRICKSON

HOOK: *Mustad 3906, Nos. 10-16.*
THREAD: *Gray.*
TAIL: *Dark blue dun hackle fibers.*
BODY: *Muskrat fur.*
HACKLE: *Dark blue dun.*
WING: *Wood duck flank.*
NOTE: *The Dark and Light Hendricksons are two wets that can save the day when the natural, Ephemerella subvaria, is on the water, but trout are refusing dry Hendricksons.*

HORNBERG

HOOK: *Mustad 9671, Nos. 6-16.*
THREAD: *Black.*
BODY: *Medium silver tinsel.*
UNDERWING: *Sparse yellow hackle fibers.*
OVERWING: *Mallard flank feather.*
HACKLE: *Brown and grizzly, mixed.*
NOTE: *This pattern is often listed as a streamer, which is correct, depending on the size and how you tie it.*

MARCH BROWN

HOOK: *Mustad 3906, Nos. 10-16.*
THREAD: *Tan.*
TAILS: *Pheasant center tail fibers.*
BODY: *Hare's ear fur.*
HACKLE: *Brown hen.*
WING: *Mallard quill.*

QUILL GORDON

HOOK: *Mustad 3906, Nos. 12-18.*
THREAD: *Tan.*
TAIL: *Wood duck flank.*
RIB: *Fine gold wire.*
BODY: *Stripped peacock quill.*
HACKLE: *Dark blue dun hen.*
WING: *Wood duck flank.*
NOTE: *This is the wet version of the famous Theodore Gordon dry fly by the same name.*

BROWN WOOLLY WORM

HOOK: *Mustad 9671, Nos. 2-14.*
THREAD: *Brown.*
TAIL: *Scarlet hackle fibers.*
HACKLE: *Grizzly, palmered.*
BODY: *Brown chenille.*
NOTE: *The Woolly Worms are superb flies for bluegills and other panfish. Tie them in the smallest sizes, and de-barb the hooks to make them easier to remove from the mouths of hungry fish.*

Soft-Hackled Wet Flies

IRON BLUE WINGLESS
HOOK: *Mustad 3906, Nos. 12-20.*
THREAD: *Red.*
TAIL: *Honey dun hackle fibers.*
BODY: *Mole's fur.*
HACKLE: *Honey dun hen.*
NOTE: *Honey dun hackle has reddish or ginger fibers with a dun center stripe.*

PARTRIDGE AND GREEN
HOOK: *Mustad 3906, Nos. 10-16.*
THREAD: *Olive.*
BODY: *Green silk floss.*
THORAX: *Mixed fur from hare's face (optional).*
HACKLE: *Gray partridge.*
NOTE: *Sylvester Nemes, in his book The Soft Hackled Fly, brought these attractive and useful dressings to our attention.*

PARTRIDGE AND YELLOW
HOOK: *Mustad 3906, Nos. 10-16.*
THREAD: *Yellow.*
BODY: *Yellow silk floss.*
THORAX: *Mixed fur from hare's face (optional).*
HACKLE: *Brown or gray partridge.*

RED HACKLE
HOOK: *Mustad 3906, Nos. 12-14.*
THREAD: *Crimson silk.*
RIB: *Narrow gold tinsel.*
BODY: *Bronze-colored peacock herl.*
HACKLE: *Red furnace.*
NOTE: *Bronze peacock herl is almost impossible to find. It's worth the digging you will have to do through fly shop herl bins.*

STARLING AND HERL
HOOK: *Mustad 3906, Nos. 10-16.*
THREAD: *Olive.*
BODY: *Peacock herl.*
HACKLE: *Covert hackle from starling wing.*

Iron Blue Wingless

March Brown Spider

Partridge and Green

Partridge and Orange

Partridge and Yellow

Pheasant Tail

Red Hackle

Snipe and Purple

Starling and Herl

Tups Indispensable

MARCH BROWN SPIDER
HOOK: *Mustad 3906, Nos. 10-16.*
THREAD: *Orange.*
RIB: *Narrow gold tinsel.*
BODY: *Mixed fur from hare's face.*
HACKLE: *Brown partridge.*
NOTE: *This is the author's very favorite fly when it comes to searching a riffle or run at a time when no insects are hatching and no trout are rising.*

PARTRIDGE AND ORANGE
HOOK: *Mustad 3906, Nos. 10-16.*
THREAD: *Orange.*
BODY: *Orange silk floss.*
THORAX: *Mixed fur from hare's face (optional).*
HACKLE: *Brown partridge.*
NOTE: *The Partridge and Green, Partridge and Orange, and Partridge and Yellow are simple to tie, and cover a spectrum of natural aquatic insects. They deserve a special compartment in your fly boxes.*

PHEASANT TAIL
HOOK: *Mustad 3906, Nos. 10-16.*
THREAD: *Brown.*
TAIL: *Pheasant center tail fibers.*
BODY: *Pheasant center tail fibers, wound with fine gold wire.*
HACKLE: *Brown or gray partridge.*
NOTE: *Pheasant tail, like peacock herl, seems to have a mysterious attraction to trout. This is a good one.*

SNIPE AND PURPLE
HOOK: *Mustad 3906, Nos. 10-16.*
THREAD: *Purple.*
BODY: *Purple silk floss.*
HACKLE: *Covert hackle from snipe wing.*

TUPS INDISPENSABLE
HOOK: *Mustad 3906, Nos. 10-16.*
THREAD: *Yellow.*
TAIL: *Blue dun hackle fibers.*
BODY: *Yellow silk floss.*
THORAX: *Light pink fur.*
HACKLE: *Blue dun hen.*
NOTE: *The body for the original British dressing was taken from the fur around the indispensable part of a ram goat's anatomy. Who thought of using it first, and why?*

Searching Nymphs

ATHERTON LIGHT
HOOK: *Mustad 3906B, Nos. 8-16.*
THREAD: *Yellow.*
TAIL: *Wood duck flank.*
RIB: *Oval gold tinsel.*
ABDOMEN: *Cream fur or synthetic.*
WINGCASE: *Dyed gold goose quill.*
THORAX: *Cream fur or synthetic.*
HACKLE: *Gray partridge.*
NOTE: *The Atherton nymphs are a perfect example of approaching a fishing situation by choosing a pattern style and varying the color of it to suit different conditions.*

ATHERTON DARK
HOOK: *Mustad 3906B, Nos. 8-16.*
THREAD: *Black.*
TAIL: *Furnace hackle fibers.*
RIB: *Oval gold tinsel.*
ABDOMEN: *Muskrat and claret seal fur, mixed.*
WINGCASE: *Dyed blue goose quill.*
THORAX: *Muskrat and claret seal fur, mixed.*
HACKLE: *Furnace, clipped top and bottom.*
NOTE: *When you first begin building your stock of fly tying materials, it is fine to substitute a material you have for one that you don't. For example, turkey quill for the blue goose.*

BREADCRUST
HOOK: *Mustad 3906, Nos. 8-16.*
THREAD: *Black.*
UNDERRIB: *Brown hackle stem.*
OVERRIB: *Gold wire, reverse wrapped.*
BODY: *Orange fur or wool yarn.*
HACKLE: *Grizzly hen.*

CAREY SPECIAL
HOOK: *Mustad 9672, Nos. 4-14.*
THREAD: *Black.*
TAIL: *Ringneck pheasant rump fibers.*
BODY: *Olive chenille.*
HACKLE: *Ringneck pheasant rump feather.*
NOTE: *The Carey Special is tied with or without tail, and with all sorts of herls, furs, yarns, and chenilles for the body. The one constant is the thick rump hackle.*

FLEDERMAUS
HOOK: *Mustad 9671, Nos. 4-12.*
THREAD: *Black.*
BODY: *Loose dubbing of muskrat fur.*
WING: *Gray squirrel tail.*

Atherton Light

Atherton Medium

Atherton Dark

Brassie

Breadcrust

Burlap

Carey Special

Casual Dress

Fledermaus

Gray Nymph

ATHERTON MEDIUM
HOOK: *Mustad 3906B, Nos. 8-16.*
THREAD: *Brown.*
TAIL: *Brown partridge fibers.*
RIB: *Oval gold tinsel.*
ABDOMEN: *Hare's ear fur.*
WINGCASE: *Dyed blue goose quill.*
THORAX: *Hare's ear fur.*
HACKLE: *Brown partridge.*

BRASSIE
HOOK: *Mustad 3906, Nos. 10-20.*
THREAD: *Black.*
ABDOMEN: *Copper wire over an underbody of floss.*
THORAX: *Muskrat fur.*

BURLAP
HOOK: *Mustad 3906B, Nos. 6-12.*
THREAD: *Brown.*
TAIL: *Moose, deer, or elk body hair.*
BODY: *Burlap.*
HACKLE: *Grizzly hen, undersized.*

CASUAL DRESS
HOOK: *Mustad 9672, Nos. 6-12.*
THREAD: *Black.*
TAIL: *Muskrat fur with guard hairs.*
ABDOMEN: *Muskrat fur twisted into dubbing rope.*
THORAX: *Muskrat fur collar with guard hairs.*
HEAD: *Black ostrich herl.*

GRAY NYMPH
HOOK: *Mustad 3906, Nos. 6-12.*
THREAD: *Gray.*
TAIL: *Grizzly hackle fibers.*
BODY: *Muskrat fur with guard hairs.*
HACKLE: *Grizzly hen.*
NOTE: *A very good searching pattern when nothing specific is going on. Weight it with 10-12 turns of lead wire to get it down near the bottom.*

GIRDLE BUG

HOOK: *Mustad 9672, Nos. 6-10.*
THREAD: *Black.*
TAIL: *White rubber hackle.*
BODY: *Black chenille.*
LEGS: *White rubber hackle.*

HERL NYMPH

HOOK: *Mustad 9671, Nos. 10-16.*
THREAD: *Black.*
BODY: *Peacock herl.*
COLLAR: *Black ostrich herl.*
LEGS: *Black hackle fibers.*

MARTINEZ BLACK

HOOK: *Mustad 3906B, Nos. 8-16.*
THREAD: *Black.*
TAIL: *Guinea feather fibers.*
RIB: *Fine copper tinsel.*
ABDOMEN: *Black seal fur.*
WINGCASE: *Bright green floss.*
THORAX: *Black chenille.*
HACKLE: *Gray partridge.*

PHEASANT TAIL

HOOK: *Mustad 3906, Nos. 10-16.*
THREAD: *Brown.*
TAIL: *Ringneck pheasant center tail fibers.*
RIB: *Gold wire.*
BODY: *Ringneck pheasant center tail fibers.*
LEGS: *Ringneck pheasant center tail fiber tips.*
NOTE: *One of the best because of its pheasant herl. Noted most for its success on spring creeks, when presented dead-drift to fussy fish.*

TELLICO

HOOK: *Mustad 3906B, Nos. 6-16.*
THREAD: *Black.*
TAIL: *Guinea feather fibers.*
SHELLBACK: *Ringneck pheasant center tail fibers.*
RIB: *Peacock herl.*
BODY: *Yellow fur or synthetic.*
HACKLE: *Brown hen.*

Girdle Bug

Gold Ribbed Hare's Ear

Herl Nymph

March Brown

Martinez Black

Muskrat

Pheasant Tail

Teeny Nymph

Tellico

Zug Bug

GOLD RIBBED HARE'S EAR

HOOK: *Mustad 3906B, Nos. 6-16.*
THREAD: *Black.*
TAIL: *Tuft of hare's poll hair.*
RIB: *Medium gold tinsel.*
ABDOMEN: *Tan fur from hare's mask.*
WINGCASE: *Brown mottled turkey.*
THORAX: *Darker fur from hare's mask, with guard.*
NOTE: *One of the very finest searching patterns. Should be carried both weighted and unweighted. Looks like a vast array of natural aquatic insects.*

MARCH BROWN

HOOK: *Mustad 3906B, Nos. 10-12.*
THREAD: *Brown.*
TAIL: *Ringneck pheasant tail fibers.*
RIB: *Brown cotton thread.*
ABDOMEN: *Red fox and amber seal fur, mixed.*
WINGCASE: *Ringneck pheasant tail fibers.*
THORAX: *Red fox and amber seal fur, mixed.*
LEGS: *Brown partridge.*

MUSKRAT

HOOK: *Mustad 38941, Nos. 6-16.*
THREAD: *Black.*
BODY: *Muskrat fur twisted into dubbing rope.*
LEGS: *Guinea feather fibers.*
HEAD: *Black ostrich herl.*
NOTE: *Originated by Polly Rosborough to imitate cranefly larvae. But it looks like a lot of other aquatic larvae, and is a good searching pattern.*

TEENY NYMPH

HOOK: *Mustad 3906B, Nos. 4-12.*
THREAD: *Brown.*
BODY: *Ringneck pheasant center tail fibers.*
LEGS: *Tips of body fibers.*

ZUG BUG

HOOK: *Mustad 3906B, Nos. 6-16.*
THREAD: *Black.*
TAIL: *Peacock herl.*
RIB: *Oval silver tinsel.*
BODY: *Peacock herl.*
HACKLE: *Furnace, sparse.*
WINGCASE: *Wood duck flank, clipped short.*
NOTE: *The Zug Bug, Gold Ribbed Hare's Ear, Gray Nymph, and Pheasant Tail cover the color spectrum of natural nymphs. These four in a range of sizes, weighted and unweighted, would start a fine nymph fly box.*

Mayfly Nymphs

BLACK DRAKE
HOOK: *Mustad 38941, Nos. 8-12.*
THREAD: *Gray.*
TAIL: *Speckled guinea fibers.*
BODY: *Beaver belly fur, with guard hairs.*
LEGS: *Speckled guinea.*
WINGCASE: *Black ostrich.*
NOTE: *A Polly Rosborough dressing, this fly has the right shape to imitate the swimmer mayfly nymphs. Fish it with the kind of movement that would suggest a swimming insect.*

EPHEMERA
HOOK: *Mustad 38941, Nos. 4-8.*
THREAD: *Brown.*
TAIL: *Tan ostrich herl tips.*
ABDOMEN: *Creamish-amber seal fur.*
WINGCASE: *Brown goose quill.*
THORAX: *Creamish-amber seal fur.*

IDA MAY
HOOK: *Partridge G3A, Nos. 8-10.*
THREAD: *Black.*
TAIL: *Grizzly fibers dyed dark green.*
UNDERRIB: *Peacock herl.*
OVERRIB: *Gold wire.*
BODY: *Black fur or yarn.*
HACKLE: *Grizzly dyed dark green.*
NOTE: *This is a Charlie Brooks pattern that matches the various nymphs of the Western Green Drake complex, in the genus* Ephemerella.

LITTLE OLIVE NYMPH
HOOK: *Mustad 3906B, Nos. 14-20.*
THREAD: *Olive.*
TAIL: *Blue dun hackle fibers.*
BODY: *Olive fur.*
HACKLE: *Blue dun hen.*
NOTE: *This is another variation of a soft-hackled wet fly tied to imitate nymphs of the* Baetis *genus.*

QUILL GORDON
HOOK: *Mustad 3906B, Nos. 12-14.*
THREAD: *Gray.*
TAIL: *Wood duck flank fibers.*
ABDOMEN: *Grayish-brown fur.*
THORAX: *Dark gray fur.*
NOTE: *The nymph of the same hatch imitated by the famous Quill Gordon dry and wet flies.*

BLUE-WING OLIVE
HOOK: *Mustad 9671, Nos. 14-20.*
THREAD: *Gray.*
TAILS: *Blue dun hackle fibers.*
BODY: *Gray seal fur.*
HACKLE: *Blue dun hen.*
NOTE: *A Rick Hafele dressing, this is a soft-hackled wet fly that can be varied in size and color to match many mayfly hatches.*

FLOATING EMERGER NYMPH
HOOK: *Mustad 94833, Nos. 12-20.*
THREAD: *Olive.*
TAILS: *Blue dun hackle fibers, split.*
BODY: *Olive fur or synthetic.*
WINGCASE: *Knot of olive or synthetic fur.*
LEGS: *Brown hackle.*
NOTE: *This nymph can be varied to match most mayfly hatches. A ball of synthetic foam encased in nylon stocking is often used for the wingcase.*

HENDRICKSON
HOOK: *Mustad 3906B, Nos. 10-12.*
THREAD: *Brown.*
TAIL: *Wood duck flank fibers.*
ABDOMEN: *Reddish-amber fur or synthetic.*
WINGCASE: *Brown goose quill.*
THORAX: *Creamish-amber fur or synthetic.*
NOTE: *This imitates the nymph of the same species matched by the Hendrickson dry and wet.*

NEAR ENOUGH
HOOK: *Mustad 38941, Nos. 8-14.*
THREAD: *Tan.*
TAIL: *Mallard flank fibers, dyed tan.*
BODY: *Gray fox fur.*
LEGS: *Mallard flank fibers, dyed tan.*
WINGCASE: *Butts of leg fibers.*
NOTE: *The Near Enough comes near enough to matching so many mayfly nymphs that it deserves its name, and a spot in your fly box.*

TIMBERLINE
HOOK: *Mustad 3906B, Nos. 12-16.*
THREAD: *Brown.*
TAIL: *Moose body hairs.*
RIB: *Copper wire.*
BODY: *Hare's ear fur.*
WINGCASE: *Ringneck pheasant center tail fibers.*
THORAX: *Hare's ear fur.*
LEGS: *Ringneck pheasant center tail fiber tips.*
NOTE: *Used primarily for hatches of mayflies in high mountain lakes.*

Black Drake

Blue-wing Olive

Ephemera

Floating Emerger Nymph

Ida May

Hendrickson

Little Olive Nymph

Near Enough

Quill Gordon

Timberline

Stonefly Nymphs

BITCH CREEK

HOOK: *Mustad 9672, Nos. 4-10.*
THREAD: *Black.*
TAILS: *White rubber hackle.*
ABDOMEN: *Black chenille with orange chenille woven belly.*
HACKLE: *Brown, palmered over thorax.*
THORAX: *Black chenille.*
ANTENNAE: *White rubber hackle.*
NOTE: *Not an exact imitation by any means, but looks like the big salmon fly nymphs, and takes a lot of big trout.*

BOX CANYON STONE

HOOK: *Eagle Claw 1197B, Nos. 2-8.*
THREAD: *Black.*
TAILS: *Brown goose quill fibers.*
ABDOMEN: *Black yarn.*
WINGCASE: *Mottled turkey quill.*
HACKLE: *Furnace, palmered over thorax.*
THORAX: *Black yarn.*
NOTE: *This is perhaps the best imitation of the giant salmon fly nymph. Most should be tied with substantial weight, and the hook is usually bent 30 degrees after the fly is tied.*

KAUFMANN'S GOLDEN STONE

HOOK: *Mustad 9575, Nos. 2-10.*
THREAD: *Orange.*
WEIGHT: *12-20 turns lead wire, flattened.*
TAIL: *Brown goose quill fibers.*
RIB: *Flat gold monofilament.*
ABDOMEN: *Orange, yellow, amber, brown seal mixed with hare's ear fur.*
WINGCASE: *Dyed gold turkey quill in three sections.*
THORAX: *Same as abdomen.*
ANTENNAE: *Brown goose quill fibers.*

TED'S STONE

HOOK: *Mustad 9672, Nos. 6-10.*
THREAD: *Black.*
TAIL: *Goose quill fibers.*
ABDOMEN: *Tobacco-brown chenille.*
WINGCASE: *Two strips body chenille.*
HACKLE: *Brown, palmered over thorax.*
THORAX: *Orange chenille.*
NOTE: *Originated by the late Ted Trueblood.*

EARLY BROWN STONE

HOOK: *Mustad 9672, Nos. 10-12.*
THREAD: *Brown.*
TAILS: *Brown goose quill fibers.*
RIB: *Flat brown monofilament.*
ABDOMEN: *Tan fur or synthetic.*
WINGCASE: *Turkey quill.*
THORAX: *Brown fur or synthetic.*
LEGS: *Brown hackle.*

Bitch Creek

Montana Stone

Box Canyon Stone

Kaufmann's Black Stone

Kaufmann's Golden Stone

Stonefly Creeper

Ted's Stone

Little Yellow Stone

Early Brown Stone

Early Black Stone

MONTANA STONE

HOOK: *Mustad 79580, Nos. 4-8.*
THREAD: *Black.*
TAIL: *Black hackle tips.*
ABDOMEN: *Black chenille.*
WINGCASE: *Black chenille.*
HACKLE: *Black, palmered over thorax.*
THORAX: *Yellow chenille.*
NOTE: *Like the Bitch Creek, not an exact imitation, but a very effective pattern.*

KAUFMANN'S BLACK STONE

HOOK: *Mustad 9575, Nos. 2-10.*
THREAD: *Black.*
WEIGHT: *12-20 turns lead wire, flattened.*
TAIL: *Black goose quill fibers.*
RIB: *Flat black monofilament.*
ABDOMEN: *Brown, claret, and black seal fur, mixed.*
WINGCASE: *Dyed black turkey quill tied in three sections.*
THORAX: *Brown, claret, and black seal fur, mixed.*
ANTENNAE: *Black goose quill fibers.*

STONEFLY CREEPER

HOOK: *Mustad 3906B, Nos. 10-12.*
THREAD: *Yellow.*
TAIL: *Two ringneck center tail fibers.*
RIB: *Ginger hackle stem.*
ABDOMEN: *Amber seal fur.*
SHELLBACK: *Wood duck flank fibers.*
THORAX: *Same as abdomen.*
HACKLE: *Brown partridge, clipped on top.*

LITTLE YELLOW STONE

HOOK: *Mustad 38941, No. 10.*
THREAD: *Light yellow.*
TAIL: *Mallard flank feathers dyed chartreuse.*
BODY: *Chartreuse dyed rabbit fur.*
LEGS: *Mallard flank dyed chartreuse.*
WINGCASE: *Mallard flank dyed chartreuse.*

EARLY BLACK STONE

HOOK: *Mustad 9672, Nos. 10-12.*
THREAD: *Black.*
TAILS: *Goose quill fibers.*
RIB: *Flat black monofilament.*
ABDOMEN: *Dark brown fur or synthetic.*
WINGCASE: *Goose quill.*
THORAX: *Black fur or synthetic.*
LEGS: *Dark blue dun hackle.*

Caddisfly Nymphs

Tied-down Caddis

Strawman

Green Rock Worm

Latex Caddis

Green Caddis Larva

Little Green Caddis

Cinnamon Sedge Pupa

Olive Sedge

Ginger Deep Sparkle Pupa

Ginger Emergent Sparkle Pupa

TIED-DOWN CADDIS

HOOK: *Mustad 3906B, Nos. 10-16.*
THREAD: *Tan.*
HACKLE: *Ginger, palmered.*
BODY: *Orange wool yarn.*
SHELLBACK: *Deer body hair.*
TAIL: *Shellback hair tied down at end of body.*
NOTE: *Leave about 8-10 inches of thread dangling at the back of the body; when you've finished everything else, draw down the wing hair and tie it down with the dangling thread.*

GREEN ROCK WORM

HOOK: *Eagle Claw 1197B, Nos. 8-12.*
THREAD: *Black.*
BODY: *Caddis green fur or synthetic.*
LEGS: *Green-dyed speckled guinea fibers.*
HEAD: *Black ostrich herl.*
NOTE: *The natural imitated by the Green Rock Worm lives only in riffles, indicating that this dressing will work best in shallow, roughened water.*

GREEN CADDIS LARVA

HOOK: *Mustad 37160, Nos. 12-18.*
THREAD: *Black.*
WEIGHT: *10-12 turns lead wire.*
ABDOMEN: *Green fur or synthetic.*
LEGS: *Grouse hackle fibers.*
THORAX: *Brown fur or synthetic.*

CINNAMON SEDGE PUPA

HOOK: *Mustad 3906, Nos. 8-10.*
THREAD: *Brown.*
ABDOMEN: *Orangish-brown fur or synthetic.*
WINGCASE: *Dark gray mallard quill sections.*
THORAX: *Dark brown fur, with guard hairs.*

GINGER DEEP SPARKLE PUPA

HOOK: *Mustad 94840, Nos. 12-18.*
THREAD: *Tan.*
WEIGHT: *8-10 turns lead wire.*
UNDERBODY: *Cream fur and amber sparkle yarn, mixed.*
OVERBODY: *Amber sparkle yarn.*
HACKLE: *Wood duck flank fibers.*
HEAD: *Cream marabou or cream fur.*
NOTE: *A Gary LaFontaine pattern, this is just a sample of many he has listed, in his fine book* Caddisflies, *to imitate the caddis pupa down on the bottom.*

STRAWMAN

HOOK: *Mustad 9671, Nos. 10-14.*
THREAD: *Brown.*
TAIL: *Mallard flank fibers.*
RIB: *Pale yellow thread.*
BODY: *Deer body hair, spun and clipped.*
HACKLE: *Partridge or hen grizzly.*
NOTE: *Originated by Paul Young to imitate caddis larvae still in their cases. Especially effective where caddis make their cases of vegetation instead of pebbles and sand: in lakes and ponds.*

LATEX CADDIS

HOOK: *Mustad 3906B, Nos. 8-18.*
THREAD: *Brown.*
WEIGHT: *10-15 turns lead wire.*
ABDOMEN: *Latex strip, wound and tinted olive.*
THORAX: *Brown rabbit fur with guard hairs.*
NOTE: *Another imitation of the green rock worms. These free-living caddis larvae cannot swim, so your dressing should be allowed to tumble along the bottom. Tint with Pantone marker.*

LITTLE GREEN CADDIS

HOOK: *Mustad 3906, Nos. 12-14.*
THREAD: *Black.*
BODY: *Insect green fur or synthetic.*
LEGS: *Blue dun hackle fibers.*
WINGCASE: *Gray mallard shoulder feathers, trimmed.*
HEAD: *Black ostrich herl.*
NOTE: *Tied to imitate the pupal stage of the caddis. The sizes and colors of this pattern can be varied to match other species of caddis.*

OLIVE SEDGE

HOOK: *Mustad 3906, Nos. 10-16.*
THREAD: *Brown.*
ABDOMEN: *Olive fur or synthetic.*
WINGCASE: *Gray mallard quill sections.*
BEARD: *Brown partridge.*
THORAX: *Hare's ear fur.*

GINGER EMERGENT SPARKLE PUPA

HOOK: *Mustad 94840, Nos. 12-18.*
THREAD: *Tan.*
UNDERBODY: *Cream fur and amber sparkle yarn, mixed.*
OVERBODY: *Amber sparkle yarn.*
WING: *Light brown deer hair.*
HEAD: *Cream marabou or cream fur.*
NOTE: *Another LaFontaine pattern that is just a sample of many color variations that he lists in* Caddisflies.

Dragonfly, Damselfly and Leech Nymphs

GREEN DAMSEL

HOOK: *Mustad 38941, Nos. 8-12.*
THREAD: *Olive.*
TAIL: *Olive marabou.*
BODY: *Pale olive rabbit fur.*
LEGS: *Teal flank dyed pale olive.*
WINGCASE: *Olive marabou one shade darker than tail.*
NOTE: *A Polly Rosborough dressing that is hard to beat when trying to imitate the difficult damselfly nymph.*

GREEN MOUNTAIN DAMSEL

HOOK: *Mustad 9672, Nos. 4-8.*
THREAD: *Olive.*
TAIL: *Olive goose quill fibers.*
RIB: *Gold wire.*
SHELLBACK: *Olive marabou.*
BODY: *Dark green seal fur.*
WINGCASE: *Olive marabou.*

RANDALL'S GREEN DRAGON

HOOK: *Eagle Claw 1206, Nos. 4-8.*
THREAD: *Olive.*
WEIGHT: *10-15 turns lead wire.*
TAIL: *Olive-dyed goose quill fibers.*
RIB: *Flat clear monofilament.*
ABDOMEN: *Olive rabbit fur and insect green seal fur, mixed.*
LEGS: *Olive goose quill fibers.*
WINGCASE: *Olive mallard quill segment.*
THORAX: *Same as body.*

BLACK WOOLLY LEECH

HOOK: *Mustad 9672, Nos. 2-6.*
THREAD: *Black.*
WEIGHT: *15-20 turns lead wire.*
TAIL: *Black marabou.*
WEED GUARD: *30-pound mono-filament.*
HACKLE: *Black, palmered.*
BODY: *Black chenille or fur.*
EYES: *Silver bead chain.*

BLACK MARABOU LEECH

HOOK: *Mustad 9672, Nos. 2-10.*
THREAD: *Black.*
WEIGHT: *10-15 turns lead wire.*
TAIL: *Black marabou.*
BODY: *Black fur.*
WING: *Black marabou.*

Green Damsel

Pheasant Rump

Green Mountain Damsel

Beaverpelt

Randall's Green Dragon

Troth Leech

Black Woolly Leech

Brown Woolly Leech

Black Marabou Leech

Hellgrammite

PHEASANT RUMP

HOOK: *Mustad 9672, Nos. 8-12.*
THREAD: *Olive.*
TAIL: *Olive marabou.*
BODY: *Fluffy underfeather from pheasant rump, dyed olive, dubbed on waxed silk.*
NOTE: *Use two or three of the under-feathers; wax your silk well and twirl the feathers onto it like fur dubbing. Leave it loose so it will work well in the water.*

BEAVERPELT

HOOK: *Mustad 3906, Nos. 8-16.*
THREAD: *Gray.*
TAIL: *Mallard flank fibers.*
BODY: *Beaver fur.*
LEGS: *Mallard flank fibers.*
NOTE: *One of the oldest dragonfly nymph dressings. Should be either crept along the bottom, or fished with short strips through the mid-depths, next to beds of vegetation.*

TROTH LEECH

HOOK: *Mustad 79580, No. 4.*
THREAD: *Black.*
TAIL: *Dark brown marabou.*
BODY: *Dark brown marabou, wound on as hackle, clipped top and bottom.*
NOTE: *One of the liveliest leech imitations. You can seldom retrieve a leech dressing too fast. There's no thrill like watching the water bulge up behind one.*

BROWN WOOLLY LEECH

HOOK: *Mustad 9672, Nos. 2-6.*
THREAD: *Brown.*
WEIGHT: *15-20 turns lead wire.*
TAIL: *Brown marabou.*
WEED GUARD: *30-pound mono-filament.*
HACKLE: *Brown, palmered.*
BODY: *Brown chenille or fur.*
EYES: *Silver bead chain.*

HELLGRAMMITE

HOOK: *Mustad 79580, Nos. 4-8.*
THREAD: *Black.*
TAILS: *Black goose quill fibers.*
RIB: *Black ostrich herl.*
ABDOMEN: *Black floss.*
WINGCASE: *Black goose quill section.*
HACKLE: *Black, palmered over thorax.*
THORAX: *Black fur with red wool breast.*
LEGS: *Black goose quill fibers.*
NOTE: *Hellgrammites live in and under the rocks of the fast sections of streams.*

Scud, Shrimp and Midge Nymphs

SCUD

HOOK: *Mustad 7957B, Nos. 8-14.*
THREAD: *Olive.*
TAIL: *Olive-dun hackle fibers.*
SHELLBACK: *4 mil plastic sheeting.*
RIBBING: *6-pound clear monofilament.*
BODY: *Grayish-olive fur.*
ANTENNAE: *Olive-dun hackle fibers.*
NOTE: *Scuds are found wherever the water is slow or still and there are plenty of weeds to hang out in. You can substitute plastic from a freezer bag for the 4 mil plastic.*

OTTER NYMPH

HOOK: *Mustad 3906, Nos. 8-14.*
THREAD: *Tan.*
TAIL: *Brown grouse.*
BODY: *Otter fur.*
LEGS: *Brown grouse.*
NOTE: *A fine Ted Trueblood pattern that represents various scuds, plus a variety of other organisms. Makes a fine searching pattern, too.*

FRESH WATER SHRIMP

HOOK: *Mustad 9253, Nos. 10-20.*
THREAD: *Black.*
SHELLBACK: *Peacock herl.*
HACKLE: *Brown, trimmed.*
BODY: *Olive wool or floss.*

WATERBOATMAN

HOOK: *Mustad 3906, Nos. 10-14.*
THREAD: *Black.*
WEIGHT: *8-10 turns lead wire.*
TAIL: *Brown partridge.*
SHELLBACK: *Metallic, bluish mallard secondary quill.*
BODY: *Red fox fur.*
LEGS: *Goose quill fibers.*
NOTE: *These little critters swim with strokes of their oar-like legs. You should twitch the fly along through the water, usually with a rhythmic throbbing of your rod tip.*

TDC MIDGE

HOOK: *Mustad 7957B, Nos. 10-16.*
THREAD: *Black.*
RIB: *Narrow silver tinsel.*
BODY: *Black wool yarn.*
THORAX: *Black chenille.*
COLLAR: *White ostrich herl.*
NOTE: *This fly imitates the pupal stage of the midge. It should be fished with little movement. A hand-twist retrieve is best. Be sure to straighten your leader to help detect takes.*

Scud

Olive Scud

Otter Nymph

Shellback Shrimp

Fresh Water Shrimp

Cress Bug

Waterboatman

Backswimmer

TDC Midge

Mosquito Larva

OLIVE SCUD

HOOK: *Mustad 7957B, Nos. 8-16.*
THREAD: *Olive.*
TAIL: *Olive hackle fibers.*
SHELLBACK: *Clear plastic.*
RIB: *Olive thread.*
BODY: *Olive-gray seal mixed with olive rabbit fur.*
LEGS: *Olive hackle.*
ANTENNAE: *Wood duck flank fibers.*

SHELLBACK SHRIMP

HOOK: *Mustad 3906, Nos. 8-14.*
THREAD: *Gray.*
TAIL: *Blue dun hackle.*
SHELLBACK: *Clear plastic cut from freezer bag.*
RIB: *Silver wire.*
BODY: *Grayish-olive synthetic dubbing.*
NOTE: *The terms shrimp and scud are generally used to refer to the same characters: crustaceans of the order Amphipoda.*

CRESS BUG

HOOK: *Mustad 3906, Nos. 10-18.*
THREAD: *Gray.*
BODY: *25% muskrat, 75% gray seal fur, mixed. Trim top, taper sides and bottom; paint top black with felt tip pen.*
NOTE: *Cress bugs, or water sowbugs, are found in slow and still waters from one coast to the other. They run around a lot but don't swim; fish your imitations very slowly.*

BACKSWIMMER

HOOK: *Mustad 7957B, Nos. 10-14.*
THREAD: *Olive.*
SHELLBACK: *Mottled turkey quill.*
LEGS: *Olive-dyed turkey quill fibers.*
BODY: *Olive tinsel chenille.*
NOTE: *Like waterboatmen, which are close relatives, backswimmers swim with oar-like movements of their legs, and should be imitated with a fly twitched through the water.*

MOSQUITO LARVA

HOOK: *Mustad 3906B, Nos. 14-18.*
THREAD: *Gray.*
TAIL: *Grizzly hackle fibers.*
BODY: *Grizzly hackle stem.*
THORAX: *Grizzly hackle, trimmed.*
FEELERS: *Grizzly hackle fibers.*

Streamers and Bucktails

GRAY GHOST
HOOK: *Mustad 9575, Nos. 4-12.*
THREAD: *Black.*
RIB: *Flat silver tinsel.*
BODY: *Orange floss.*
UNDERWING: *White bucktail.*
OVERWING: *Four gray saddle hackles.*
THROAT: *White bucktail/four peacock herls/golden pheasant crest.*
SHOULDER: *Silver pheasant body feather.*
CHEEK: *Jungle cock or substitute.*

SUPERVISOR
HOOK: *Mustad 9575, Nos. 2-12.*
THREAD: *Black.*
TAIL: *Red wool yarn.*
RIB: *Oval silver tinsel.*
BODY: *Flat silver tinsel.*
UNDERWING: *White bucktail.*
OVERWING: *Four light-blue saddle hackles.*
TOPPING: *Four to six strands peacock herl.*
THROAT: *White hackle fibers.*
SHOULDER: *Pale green hackle tips.*
CHEEK: *Jungle cock or substitute.*

BLACK NOSE DACE
HOOK: *Mustad 9575, Nos. 6-14.*
THREAD: *Black.*
TAIL: *Red wool yarn.*
BODY: *Embossed silver tinsel.*
UNDERWING: *White bucktail.*
MID-WING: *Black bear hair.*
OVERWING: *Brown bucktail.*

LITTLE RAINBOW TROUT
HOOK: *Mustad 9575, Nos. 4-14.*
THREAD: *Black.*
TAIL: *Bright green bucktail.*
RIB: *Flat silver tinsel.*
BODY: *Pale pink fur.*
THROAT: *Pink bucktail.*
WING: *Equal amounts white, pink and bright green bucktail, topped with badger hair or gray squirrel tail.*
CHEEK: *Jungle cock.*

LITTLE BROWN TROUT
HOOK: *Mustad 9575, Nos. 4-14.*
THREAD: *Black.*
TAIL: *Bronze ringneck pheasant breast feather.*
RIB: *Copper wire.*
BODY: *Cream fur.*
WING: *Equal amounts yellow bucktail, reddish-orange bucktail, gray squirrel tail, red squirrel tail.*
CHEEK: *Jungle cock.*

BLACK GHOST
HOOK: *Mustad 9575, Nos. 8-12.*
THREAD: *Black.*
TAIL: *Yellow hackle fibers.*
RIB: *Flat silver tinsel.*
BODY: *Black floss.*
WING: *Four white saddle hackles.*
THROAT: *Yellow hackle.*
CHEEK: *Jungle cock or substitute.*

SPRUCE
HOOK: *Mustad 9672, Nos. 2-10.*
THREAD: *Black.*
TAIL: *Peacock sword.*
BODY: *Red floss/peacock herl.*
WING: *Two badger saddle hackles.*
HACKLE: *Badger.*

MICKEY FINN
HOOK: *Mustad 9575, Nos. 2-12.*
THREAD: *Black.*
BODY: *Embossed silver tinsel.*
UNDERWING: *Yellow bucktail.*
MID-WING: *Red bucktail.*
OVERWING: *Yellow bucktail, equal amount to underwing and mid-wing combined.*

LITTLE BROOK TROUT
HOOK: *Mustad 9575, Nos. 4-14.*
THREAD: *Black.*
TAIL: *Red floss/bright green bucktail.*
RIB: *Flat silver tinsel.*
BODY: *Cream fur.*
THROAT: *Orange bucktail.*
WING: *Equal amounts white bucktail, orange bucktail, bright green bucktail, topped with badger hair or gray squirrel.*
CHEEK: *Jungle cock.*

ROYAL COACHMAN BUCKTAIL
HOOK: *Mustad 9575, Nos. 4-10.*
THREAD: *Brown.*
TAIL: *Golden pheasant tippets.*
BODY: *Peacock herl/red floss/peacock herl.*
HACKLE: *Brown.*
WING: *White calf tail.*

Gray Ghost

Black Ghost

Supervisor

Spruce

Black Nose Dace

Mickey Finn

Little Rainbow Trout

Little Brook Trout

Little Brown Trout

Royal Coachman Bucktail

MUDDLER MINNOW

HOOK: *Mustad 9672, Nos. 1/0-12.*
THREAD: *Brown.*
TAIL: *Mottled turkey quill.*
BODY: *Flat gold tinsel.*
UNDERWING: *Gray squirrel tail.*
OVERWING: *Mottled turkey quill.*
HACKLE: *Deer hair, tied in as collar.*
HEAD: *Deer hair, spun and clipped.*

YELLOW MARABOU STREAMER

HOOK: *Mustad 9672, Nos. 4-10.*
THREAD: *Yellow.*
TAIL: *Scarlet hackle fibers.*
BODY: *Silver tinsel chenille.*
THROAT: *Scarlet hackle fibers.*
WING: *Yellow marabou.*
TOPPING: *Four to six strands peacock herl.*

OLIVE MATUKA SCULPIN

HOOK: *Mustad 9672, Nos. 2-4.*
THREAD: *Olive.*
RIB: *Gold wire.*
BODY: *Cream yarn over tapered underbody.*
WING: *Four or six olive-dun dyed grizzly hackles, tied down with ribbing wire.*
COLLAR: *Deer hair dyed dark olive.*
UNDERHEAD: *Heavy lead wire covered with art foam.*
HEAD: *Olive-dyed hare's ear fur.*

OLIVE MATUKA

HOOK: *Mustad 79580, Nos. 4-10.*
THREAD: *Olive.*
RIB: *Oval gold tinsel.*
BODY: *Olive rabbit fur.*
WINGS: *Olive-dyed grizzly hackles.*
HACKLE: *Olive-dyed grizzly.*

OLIVE WOOLLY BUGGER

HOOK: *Mustad 9672, Nos. 2-10.*
THREAD: *Olive.*
WEIGHT: *12-15 turns lead wire.*
TAIL: *Olive marabou.*
HACKLE: *Brown, palmered.*
BODY: *Olive chenille.*

Muddler Minnow

Black Marabou Muddler

Yellow Marabou Streamer

Spuddler

Olive Matuka Sculpin

Whitlock Sculpin

Olive Matuka

Zonker

Olive Woolly Bugger

Black Woolly Bugger

BLACK MARABOU MUDDLER

HOOK: *Mustad 9672, Nos. 4-10.*
THREAD: *Black.*
TAIL: *Scarlet hackle fibers.*
BODY: *Silver tinsel chenille.*
UNDERWING: *Gray squirrel tail.*
OVERWING: *Black marabou.*
HACKLE: *Deer hair, tied in as a collar.*
HEAD: *Deer hair, spun and clipped.*

SPUDDLER

HOOK: *Mustad 9672, Nos. 2-10.*
THREAD: *Brown.*
TAIL: *Brown calf tail.*
BODY: *Cream fur/red fur.*
UNDERWING: *Brown calf tail.*
OVERWING: *Four brown-dyed grizzly saddles.*
SIDEWINGS: *Red squirrel tail.*
COLLAR: *Brown antelope hair.*
HEAD: *Brown antelope hair, spun and clipped.*

WHITLOCK SCULPIN

HOOK: *Mustad 9672, Nos. 1/0-8.*
THREAD: *Light orange.*
WEIGHT: *15-20 turns lead wire.*
RIB: *Oval gold tinsel.*
BODY: *Amber seal, yellow seal, tan fox, white rabbit, mixed.*
UNDERWING: *Red fox squirrel tail.*
WING: *Two dark cree neck hackles, tinted golden brown or golden olive.*
GILLS: *Red wool.*
PECTORAL FINS: *Mallard breast.*
COLLAR: *Deer body hair.*
HEAD: *Deer body hair, spun and clipped.*

ZONKER

HOOK: *Mustad 9672, Nos. 2-8.*
THREAD: *Black.*
WEIGHT: *15-20 turns lead wire.*
BODY: *Mylar piping.*
WING: *Rabbit fur strip.*
HACKLE: *Grizzly.*
BUTT: *Red thread, used to tie down both wing and body.*

BLACK WOOLLY BUGGER

HOOK: *Mustad 9672, Nos. 2-10.*
THREAD: *Black.*
WEIGHT: *12-15 turns lead wire.*
TAIL: *Black marabou.*
HACKLE: *Black, palmered.*
BODY: *Black chenille.*

Summer Steelhead Flies

BRAD'S BRAT
HOOK: *Mustad 36890, Nos. 2-8.*
THREAD: *Black.*
TAG: *Gold tinsel.*
TAIL: *Orange and white hackle fibers, mixed.*
RIB: *Flat gold tinsel.*
BODY: *Orange wool/red wool.*
HACKLE: *Brown.*
UNDERWING: *White calf tail.*
OVERWING: *Orange calf tail.*
NOTE: *There is a great deal of overlap between summer and winter steelhead flies. Use this in sizes 4-8 for summer fish, sizes 2/0 to 4 for winter fish.*

FREIGHT TRAIN
HOOK: *Mustad 36890, Nos. 2-8.*
THREAD: *Black.*
TAIL: *Purple hackle fibers.*
RIB: *Oval silver tinsel.*
BODY: *Rear 1/4 fluorescent orange floss; second 1/4 fluorescent red floss; front half black chenille.*
HACKLE: *Purple.*
WING: *White calf tail.*

GREEN BUTT SKUNK
HOOK: *Mustad 36890, Nos. 2-8.*
THREAD: *Black.*
TAIL: *Scarlet hackle fibers.*
BUTT: *Fluorescent green chenille.*
RIB: *Oval silver tinsel.*
BODY: *Black chenille.*
HACKLE: *Black.*
WING: *White calf tail.*

MAX CANYON
HOOK: *Mustad 36890, Nos. 2-8.*
THREAD: *Black.*
TAIL: *Orange and white hackle fibers, mixed*
RIB: *Oval silver tinsel.*
BODY: *Rear 1/3 orange wool yarn; front 2/3 black wool yarn.*
HACKLE: *Black.*
UNDERWING: *White calf tail.*
OVERWING: *Orange calf tail.*

PURPLE PERIL
HOOK: *Mustad 36890, Nos. 2-8.*
THREAD: *Black.*
TAG: *Oval silver tinsel.*
TAIL: *Purple hackle fibers.*
RIB: *Oval silver tinsel.*
BODY: *Purple chenille.*
HACKLE: *Purple.*
WING: *Fox squirrel tail.*

Brad's Brat
Fall Favorite
Freight Train
Skunk
Green Butt Skunk
Kalama Special
Max Canyon
Patricia
Purple Peril
Skykomish Sunrise

FALL FAVORITE
HOOK: *Mustad 36890, Nos. 2-8.*
THREAD: *Black.*
BODY: *Silver tinsel.*
HACKLE: *Scarlet.*
WING: *Hot orange calf tail or polar bear hair.*

SKUNK
HOOK: *Mustad 36890, Nos. 2-8.*
THREAD: *Black.*
TAIL: *Scarlet hackle fibers.*
RIB: *Oval silver tinsel.*
BODY: *Black chenille.*
HACKLE: *Black.*
WING: *White calf tail.*
NOTE: *This is the most popular summer steelhead fly. It accounts for more fish in more places than any other dressing.*

KALAMA SPECIAL
HOOK: *Mustad 36890, Nos. 4-8.*
THREAD: *Black.*
TAIL: *Scarlet hackle fibers.*
HACKLE: *Golden badger, palmered.*
BODY: *Yellow wool yarn.*
WING: *White bucktail.*

PATRICIA
HOOK: *Mustad 36890, Nos. 2-8.*
THREAD: *Black.*
TAG: *Oval gold tinsel.*
TAIL: *Claret hackle fibers.*
RIB: *Oval gold tinsel.*
BODY: *Claret seal fur or goat.*
HACKLE: *Claret.*
WING: *White calf tail or polar bear hair.*

SKYKOMISH SUNRISE
HOOK: *Mustad 36890, Nos. 2-12.*
THREAD: *Black.*
TAIL: *Scarlet and yellow hackle fibers, mixed.*
RIB: *Silver tinsel.*
BODY: *Red chenille.*
HACKLE: *Scarlet and yellow, mixed.*
WING: *White calf tail or polar bear.*
NOTE: *As with most of the bright summer steelhead flies, it is also tied in larger sizes for winter steelhead. The smallest sizes also work well for sea-run cutthroat trout.*

PATRIOT

HOOK: *Mustad 36890, Nos. 2-6.*
THREAD: *Black.*
TAIL: *Scarlet hackle fibers.*
RIB: *Oval silver tinsel.*
BODY: *Yellow floss, thin.*
HACKLE: *Vivid blue saddle hackle.*
WING: *White polar bear (substitute white calf tail).*
NOTE: *Originated by Frank Amato, the Patriot fishes well for summer steelhead in Alaska, British Columbia, Washington and Oregon.*

JUICY BUG

HOOK: *Mustad 3582C, Nos. 6-10.*
THREAD: *Black.*
TAIL: *Scarlet hackle fibers.*
RIB: *Oval silver tinsel.*
BODY: *Rear half black chenille; front half red chenille.*
WING: *White calf tail, tied upright and split.*
CHEEKS: *Jungle cock (optional).*
NOTE: *Developed for the Rogue River. Erratic on the swing, and creates a great disturbance, perhaps angering the fish into striking.*

WASHOUGAL OLIVE

HOOK: *Mustad 36890, Nos. 4-8.*
THREAD: *Black.*
TAIL: *Golden-olive dyed calf tail.*
BODY: *Gold tinsel.*
BEARD: *Golden-olive dyed calf tail.*
WING: *White calf tail.*
NOTE: *Developed for his favorite Washougal River runs by the famous dry line steelhead fisherman, Bill McMillan.*

STEELHEAD BEE

HOOK: *Mustad 90240, Nos. 6-12.*
THREAD: *Black.*
WINGS: *Red fox squirrel, divided.*
TAIL: *Red fox squirrel tail.*
BODY: *Brown yarn/yellow yarn/ brown yarn or fur.*
HACKLE: *Brown hen, sparse.*
NOTE: *Originated by the famous author Roderick Haig-Brown, the Steelhead Bee is designed to ride in the surface film rather than on top of it.*

STEELHEAD MUDDLER

HOOK: *Mustad 36890, Nos. 2-10.*
THREAD: *Black.*
BODY: *Flat gold tinsel.*
UNDERWING: *Gray squirrel tail.*
OVERWING: *Mottled turkey quill.*
COLLAR: *Deer body hair.*
HEAD: *Deer hair, spun and clipped.*

Patriot

Street Walker

Juicy Bug

Umpqua Special

Washougal Olive

October Caddis

Steelhead Bee

Steelhead Caddis

Steelhead Muddler

Grease Liner

STREET WALKER

HOOK: *Eagle Claw 1197N, Nos. 2-8.*
THREAD: *Black.*
TAIL: *Purple hackle fibers.*
RIB: *Oval silver tinsel.*
BODY: *Purple chenille.*
HACKLE: *Purple saddle hackle.*
WING: *Clear flashabou.*
NOTE: *Originated by Gordon Nash. A few strands of flashabou can be added to the wings of any of the listed flies.*

UMPQUA SPECIAL

HOOK: *Eagle Claw 1197B, Nos. 2-8.*
THREAD: *Red.*
TAIL: *White hackle fibers.*
RIB: *Oval silver tinsel.*
BODY: *Rear half yellow wool yarn; front half red chenille.*
HACKLE: *Brown.*
WING: *White calf tail.*

OCTOBER CADDIS

HOOK: *Mustad 90240, Nos. 4-10.*
THREAD: *Black.*
WING: *Brown squirrel tail, divided.*
TAIL: *Golden pheasant crest.*
BODY: *Orange fur or synthetic.*
HACKLE: *Brown.*
NOTE: *Originated by conservationist Bill Bakke, executive director of Oregon Trout. Especially enticing when used with a riffling hitch.*

STEELHEAD CADDIS

HOOK: *Mustad 90240, Nos. 4-12.*
THREAD: *Black.*
BODY: *Rabbit fur.*
WING: *Brown turkey quill.*
COLLAR: *Deer body hair.*
HEAD: *Deer body hair, spun and clipped.*

GREASE LINER

HOOK: *Mustad 90240, Nos. 4-8.*
THREAD: *Black.*
TAIL: *Dark deer hair.*
BODY: *Black seal fur.*
BEARD: *Sparse grizzly.*
WING: *Dark deer hair.*
HEAD: *Spun and clipped deer hair (top half only).*

Winter Steelhead Flies

BABINE SPECIAL

HOOK: *Mustad 36890, Nos. 2-8.*
THREAD: *Red.*
WEIGHT: *12-20 turns lead wire.*
BODY: *Fluorescent red or orange chenille.*
CENTER HACKLE: *Red.*
FRONT HACKLE: *White.*
NOTE: *Just as there is much overlap between summer and winter steelhead flies, there is also much overlap between winter steelhead flies and flies used to fish for salmon.*

GOLDEN GIRL

HOOK: *Partridge down eye salmon, Nos. 5/0-4.*
THREAD: *Black.*
TAIL: *Orange hackle fibers.*
BODY: *Flat gold tinsel.*
HACKLE: *Orange saddle.*
WING: *Orange polar bear enveloped by two whole golden pheasant tippet feathers.*

POLAR SHRIMP

HOOK: *Eagle Claw 1197B, Nos. 2-8.*
THREAD: *White.*
TAIL: *Scarlet hackle fibers.*
BODY: *Orange chenille.*
HACKLE: *Orange.*
WING: *White calf tail.*

ORANGE HERON

HOOK: *Partridge single low water, Nos. 5/0-2.*
THREAD: *Red.*
RIB: *Oval silver tinsel.*
BODY HACKLE: *Pheasant rump or coot body feather, palmered.*
BODY: *Rear 2/3 orange floss; front 1/3 orange seal fur.*
BEARD: *Teal flank.*
WING: *Four fire-orange hackle tips.*
NOTE: *One of the graceful Spey flies originated by the late Syd Glasso. They were originally tied with heron feathers, but that is illegal now, and the substitutes are just as good.*

WINTER'S HOPE

HOOK: *Partridge single salmon, Nos. 5/0-2.*
THREAD: *Orange.*
BODY: *Flat silver tinsel.*
UNDER HACKLE: *Pale blue.*
OVER HACKLE: *Vivid purple.*
UNDER WING: *Two yellow hackle tips.*
OVERWING: *Two orange hackle tips.*
TOPPING: *Golden olive calf tail or golden pheasant crest.*

Babine Special

Black Boss

Golden Girl

Silver Comet

Polar Shrimp

Thor

Orange Heron

Golden Demon

Winter's Hope

Paint Brush

BLACK BOSS

HOOK: *Mustad 36890, Nos. 2-6.*
THREAD: *Orange.*
WEIGHT: *12-20 turns lead wire.*
TAG: *Flat silver tinsel.*
TAIL: *Orange calf tail.*
RIB: *Oval silver tinsel.*
BODY: *Black chenille.*
HACKLE: *Orange.*
EYES: *Bead chain.*
NOTE: *The similar Orange Boss is tied with an orange body and black hackle.*

SILVER COMET

HOOK: *Mustad 36890, Nos. 2-8.*
THREAD: *Red.*
WEIGHT: *12-20 turns lead wire.*
TAIL: *Orange calf tail.*
BODY: *Flat silver tinsel.*
HACKLE: *Orange and yellow, mixed.*
EYES: *Bead chain.*
NOTE: *Comets are also tied in black, gold, orange, brown, and yellow.*

THOR

HOOK: *Eagle Claw 1197B, Nos. 2-8.*
THREAD: *Black.*
TAIL: *Orange hackle fibers.*
BODY: *Red chenille.*
HACKLE: *Brown.*
WING: *White calf tail.*
NOTE: *Although weight is not listed in many of the dressings, it is an option you should consider, depending on the water you will fish, for many of your winter steelhead and salmon flies.*

GOLDEN DEMON

HOOK: *Mustad 36890, Nos. 2-8.*
THREAD: *Black.*
TAIL: *Golden pheasant crest feather.*
RIB: *Oval gold tinsel.*
BODY: *Flat gold tinsel.*
THROAT: *Hot orange.*
WING: *Brown bear hair or red squirrel tail.*
CHEEK: *Jungle cock or substitute.*

PAINT BRUSH

HOOK: *Mustad 7970, Nos. 2-6.*
THREAD: *Orange.*
BODY: *Flat gold tinsel palmered with orange saddle hackle.*
UNDER HACKLE: *Pale blue saddle.*
OVER HACKLE: *Vivid purple saddle.*
NOTE: *The Winter's Hope and Paint Brush are two Bill McMillan ties, designed to fish deep with dry lines and unweighted flies.*

Salmon Flies

DOUBLE EGG SPERM FLY

HOOK: *Eagle Claw 1197B, Nos. 2-8.*
THREAD: *Fluorescent red.*
BUTT: *Fluorescent orange chenille.*
BODY: *Flat silver tinsel.*
SHOULDER: *Fluorescent orange chenille.*
WING: *White marabou.*
NOTE: *The flies listed in this section are effective for Pacific salmon on the West Coast and for the same species where they have been transplanted to the Great Lakes.*

WHITE GLO-BUG

HOOK: *Mustad 9174, Nos. 4-8.*
THREAD: *White.*
BODY: *White Glo-Bug yarn.*
NOTE: *To tie this and the following Glo-Bug, tie 2-3 strands of Glo-Bug yarn to the center of the hook. Make several confining wraps in front and back of the yarn. Tie it down hard in the center. Then pull the yarn straight up and clip it on an arc. It will flare into an egg shape.*

ORANGE BOSS

HOOK: *Mustad 36890, Nos. 2-6.*
THREAD: *Orange.*
WEIGHT: *12-20 turns lead wire.*
TAG: *Flat silver tinsel.*
TAIL: *Black calf tail.*
RIB: *Oval silver tinsel.*
BODY: *Orange chenille.*
HACKLE: *Black.*
EYES: *Bead chain.*
NOTE: *There are many variations to this fly. Like most salmon flies, it is often heavily weighted, at the tier's discretion.*

BRIGHT ROE

HOOK: *Mustad 36890, Nos. 2-8.*
THREAD: *Fluorescent fire-orange.*
RIB: *Oval silver tinsel.*
BODY: *Fluorescent orange chenille.*
WING: *Fluorescent orange nylon tow yarn.*

FLASHABOU EUPHAUSID

HOOK: *Mustad 34007, Nos. 4-10.*
THREAD: *White.*
TAIL: *Pearl flashabou.*
BODY: *Braided pearl flashabou.*
THROAT: *Pearl flashabou.*
NOTE: *Another fly designed for fishing in salt water.*

Double Egg Sperm Fly

Green Wienie

White Glo-Bug

Red Glo-Bug

Orange Boss

Spade

Bright Roe

Green Amphipod

Flashabou Euphausid

Coho Blue

GREEN WIENIE

HOOK: *Mustad 36890, Nos. 2-8.*
THREAD: *Fluorescent green.*
TAIL: *Black calf tail.*
BODY: *Silver diamond braid.*
SHOULDER: *Fluorescent green chenille.*
HACKLE: *Fluorescent green saddle.*
EYES: *Bead chain.*

RED GLO-BUG

HOOK: *Mustad 9174, Nos. 4-8.*
THREAD: *Red.*
BODY: *Fluorescent red Glo-Bug yarn.*
NOTE: *See the note about the White Glo-Bug for the magic in tying this fly.*

SPADE

HOOK: *Mustad 36890, Nos. 1/0-6.*
THREAD: *Black.*
TAIL: *Dark deer hair.*
BODY: *Black chenille.*
HACKLE: *Grizzly saddle.*
NOTE: *Originated by Harry Hendrickson, member of the Anglers Club of Portland, this simple fly is very effective for salmon.*

GREEN AMPHIPOD

HOOK: *Mustad 37140, Nos. 4-8.*
THREAD: *Black.*
TAIL: *Deer body hair.*
RIB: *Working thread and two blue dun hackles, palmered.*
BODY: *Fluorescent green chenille.*
SHELLBACK: *Butts of tail fibers.*
NOTE: *Listed in* Fly Fishing for Pacific Salmon, *this dressing is tied to take salmon in salt water.*

COHO BLUE

HOOK: *Mustad 92608, Nos. 3/0-6.*
THREAD: *Black.*
TAIL: *Two light blue hackle tips.*
BODY: *Flat silver tinsel.*
WING: *White polar bear under blue polar bear (or substitute); two light blue hackles over two badger hackles enveloping the polar bear.*

Atlantic Salmon Flies

BLACK BEAR GREEN BUTT

HOOK: *Mustad 36890, Nos. 2-10.*
THREAD: *Black.*
TAG: *Flat silver tinsel.*
TAIL: *Golden pheasant crest.*
BUTT: *Fluorescent green floss.*
RIB: *Flat silver tinsel.*
BODY: *Black floss.*
THROAT: *Black hackle fibers.*
WING: *Black fitchtail (substitute black-dyed squirrel tail).*

LADY CAROLINE

HOOK: *Partridge low water, Nos. 3/0-4.*
THREAD: *Black.*
TAIL: *Reddish-brown golden pheasant breast.*
RIBBING: *Flat gold tinsel and oval silver tinsel.*
BODY HACKLE: *Pheasant rump or coot body feather.*
BODY: *Olive-green and brown seal fur, mixed.*
THROAT: *Reddish-brown golden pheasant breast.*
WING: *Bronze mallard flank.*

GREEN HIGHLANDER

HOOK: *Mustad 36890, Nos. 2/0-10.*
THREAD: *Black.*
TAG: *Bright yellow floss.*
TAIL: *Golden pheasant crest and black-barred wood duck.*
BUTT: *Black ostrich herl.*
RIB: *Oval silver tinsel; green hackle.*
BODY: *Rear 1/3 yellow floss; front 2/3 bright green seal fur.*
THROAT: *Yellow.*
UNDERWING: *Golden pheasant tippets, in strands.*
MID-WING: *Green bucktail.*
OVERWING: *White-tipped gray squirrel tail.*

RUSTY RAT

HOOK: *Mustad 36890, Nos. 2-8.*
THREAD: *Red.*
TAG: *Flat gold tinsel.*
TAIL: *Peacock sword.*
BODY: *Rear half orange floss; front half peacock herl with strands of orange floss protruding from middle.*
WING: *Gray squirrel tail.*
HACKLE: *Grizzly.*

ROYAL WULFF

HOOK: *Mustad 90240, Nos. 4-12.*
THREAD: *Black.*
WING: *White calf tail, upright and divided.*
TAIL: *White calf tail.*
BODY: *Peacock herl/red floss/peacock herl.*
HACKLE: *Coachman brown.*

Black Bear Green Butt

Blue Charm

Lady Caroline

Cosseboom

Green Highlander

Jock Scott

Rusty Rat

Thunder and Lightning

Royal Wulff

Bomber

BLUE CHARM

HOOK: *Mustad 36890, Nos. 2-10.*
THREAD: *Black.*
TIP: *Flat silver tinsel.*
TAG: *Bright yellow floss.*
TAIL: *Golden pheasant crest.*
RIB: *Flat silver tinsel.*
BODY: *Black floss.*
THROAT: *Bright blue hackle fibers.*
WING: *Bronze mallard flank.*
TOPPING: *Golden pheasant crest.*

COSSEBOOM

HOOK: *Mustad 36890, Nos. 1/0-10.*
THREAD: *Red.*
TAG: *Embossed silver tinsel.*
TAIL: *Light olive floss.*
RIB: *Embossed silver tinsel.*
BODY: *Light olive floss.*
WING: *Gray squirrel tail.*
HACKLE: *Lemon yellow.*

JOCK SCOTT

HOOK: *Mustad 36890, Nos. 2/0-10.*
THREAD: *Black.*
TAG: *Yellow floss.*
TAIL: *Golden pheasant crest and Indian crow.*
BUTT: *Black ostrich herl.*
BODY: *Yellow floss ribbed with oval silver tinsel. Black ostrich herl. Black floss ribbed with flat silver tinsel and black hackle.*
THROAT: *Guinea.*
UNDERWING: *Blue, red, and yellow bucktail, mixed.*
OVERWING: *Brown bucktail.*
CHEEKS: *Jungle cock or substitute.*

THUNDER AND LIGHTNING

HOOK: *Mustad 36890, Nos. 2-10.*
THREAD: *Black.*
TIP: *Flat gold tinsel.*
TAG: *Bright yellow floss.*
TAIL: *Golden pheasant crest and Indian crow.*
BUTT: *Black ostrich herl.*
RIB: *Oval gold tinsel.*
BODY HACKLE: *Deep orange.*
BODY: *Black floss.*
HACKLE: *Guinea dyed blue.*
WING: *Bronze mallard flank.*
TOPPING: *Golden pheasant crest.*
CHEEKS: *Jungle cock or substitute.*

BOMBER

HOOK: *Partridge salmon down eye S.E.B. Nos. 2-8.*
THREAD: *Black.*
TAIL: *White calf tail.*
HACKLE: *Grizzly, palmered.*
BODY: *Deer body hair, spun and clipped.*
WING: *White calf tail.*

Sea-run Cutthroat Flies

BORDEN SPECIAL
HOOK: *Mustad 3906, Nos. 4-8.*
THREAD: *Black.*
TAIL: *Fluorescent pink and yellow hackle fibers, mixed.*
RIB: *Silver tinsel.*
BODY: *Hareline No. 04 fluorescent pink dubbing.*
WING: *White arctic fox tail.*
UNDERHACKLE: *Yellow.*
OVERHACKLE: *Fluorescent pink.*

CUTTHROAT
HOOK: *Mustad 36890, Nos. 4-8.*
THREAD: *Yellow.*
TAG: *Flat silver tinsel.*
TAIL: *Scarlet hackle fibers.*
RIB: *Flat silver tinsel.*
BODY: *Yellow wool yarn.*
BEARD: *Red.*
UNDERWING: *Red bucktail.*
OVERWING: *White bucktail.*

GRAY HACKLE YELLOW
HOOK: *Mustad 3906, Nos. 4-8.*
THREAD: *Black.*
TAIL: *Scarlet hackle fibers.*
BODY: *Yellow floss.*
HACKLE: *Grizzly hen.*

PURPLE JOE
HOOK: *Mustad 36890, Nos. 4-10.*
THREAD: *Black.*
TAIL: *Scarlet hackle fibers.*
BUTT: *Hot orange floss.*
BODY: *Purple chenille.*
HACKLE: *Gold or silver badger.*
WINGS: *Gold or silver badger hackles.*
NOTE: *Another regional fly, the Purple Joe is considered just the ticket on Northwest Oregon rivers.*

SPRUCE FLY
HOOK: *Mustad 36890, Nos. 4-10.*
THREAD: *Black.*
TAIL: *Peacock sword.*
BUTT: *Red floss.*
BODY: *Peacock herl.*
HACKLE: *Gold or silver badger.*
WINGS: *Gold or silver badger hackles.*

Borden Special

Bucktail Coachman

Cutthroat

Gray Hackle Peacock

Gray Hackle Yellow

Knudson's Spider

Purple Joe

Skagit Cutthroat

Spruce Fly

Spider Spruce

BUCKTAIL COACHMAN
HOOK: *Mustad 3906, Nos. 4-10.*
THREAD: *Black.*
TAIL: *Scarlet hackle fibers.*
BODY: *Peacock herl.*
HACKLE: *Coachman brown.*
WING: *White bucktail.*
NOTE: *Many standard trout wet flies, bucktails, and streamers work well for sea-run cutts. So do a lot of steelhead and salmon flies, usually in the smaller sizes.*

GRAY HACKLE PEACOCK
HOOK: *Mustad 3906, Nos. 4-8.*
THREAD: *Black.*
TAIL: *Scarlet hackle fibers.*
BODY: *Peacock herl.*
HACKLE: *Grizzly hen.*
NOTE: *Many sea-run flies are considered regional; some are used only on specific rivers, and those who use them there assume no others will work. This fly is a favorite in Southwest Washington.*

KNUDSON'S SPIDER
HOOK: *Mustad 3906, Nos. 2-10.*
THREAD: *Black.*
TAIL: *Mallard flank fibers.*
BODY: *Yellow chenille.*
UNDERHACKLE: *Grizzly.*
OVERHACKLE: *Mallard flank.*

SKAGIT CUTTHROAT
HOOK: *Mustad 36890, Nos. 4-10.*
THREAD: *Red.*
TAIL: *Scarlet and orange hackle fibers, mixed.*
BUTT: *Fluorescent orange chenille.*
BODY: *Oval silver tinsel.*
INNER WING: *White bucktail.*
OUTER WING: *Scarlet goose quill.*

SPIDER SPRUCE
HOOK: *Mustad 90240, Nos. 6-10.*
THREAD: *Black.*
TAIL: *Peacock sword.*
BUTT: *Hot orange floss.*
RIB: *Gold badger hackle, palmered.*
BODY: *Peacock herl.*
HACKLE: *Green-dyed mallard or teal flank.*

Alaska Flies

Alaska Mary Ann
Alaskan Smolt
Black Matuka
Blue Smolt
Red Russian River Coho
Katmai Smolt
Kenai Connection
Little Chinook
Pixie's Revenge
Showgirl

ALASKA MARY ANN

HOOK: *Eagle Claw 1197G, Nos. 4-6.*
THREAD: *Black.*
TAIL: *Red floss.*
RIB: *Flat silver tinsel.*
BODY: *Ivory floss.*
WING: *Polar bear hair.*
CHEEKS: *Jungle cock or substitute.*
NOTE: *Many patterns listed in other parts of the book are used extensively in Alaska. The Muddler, Marabou Muddlers, Woolly Buggers, and other large streamer-type flies are very popular.*

BLACK MATUKA

HOOK: *Mustad 9575, Nos. 2-8.*
THREAD: *Black.*
WEIGHT: *12-20 turns lead wire.*
RIB: *Silver oval tinsel.*
BODY: *Black wool.*
WING: *Black hackle tied matuka style.*
HACKLE: *Black.*
NOTE: *The Olive Matuka is also very popular in Alaska.*

RED RUSSIAN RIVER COHO

HOOK: *Mustad 36717, Nos. 2-6.*
THREAD: *Black.*
UNDERWING: *White bucktail.*
OVERWING: *Red bucktail.*
NOTE: *There are many wing variations to this dressing. Another popular one calls for an orange bucktail underwing and red bucktail overwing.*

KENAI CONNECTION

HOOK: *Eagle Claw 1197G, Nos. 1/0-6.*
THREAD: *Fluorescent chartreuse.*
TAIL: *Red hackle.*
RIB: *Gold tinsel.*
BODY: *Fluorescent chartreuse chenille.*
THROAT: *Red hackle.*
WING: *White marabou.*
TOPPING: *Peacock herl.*
EYE: *Jungle cock or substitute.*

PIXIE'S REVENGE

HOOK: *Mustad 3407, No. 1/0.*
THREAD: *Fluorescent red.*
WING: *White marabou.*
OVERWING: *Silver flashabou.*
COLLAR: *Cerise saddle hackle.*
NOTE: *This is one of George Cook's Alaskabou patterns, which may be the hottest flies for Alaska waters.*

ALASKAN SMOLT

HOOK: *Mustad 9575, Nos. 2-6.*
THREAD: *Black.*
WEIGHT: *12-20 turns lead wire.*
TAIL: *Silver mylar tubing strands.*
BODY: *Silver mylar tubing tied with fluorescent orange thread.*
UNDERWING: *White bucktail.*
OVERWING: *Green bucktail.*
TOPPING: *Mallard flank fibers.*
THROAT: *Red calf tail.*
NOTE: *This fly is listed in* Fly Patterns of Alaska, *which gives dressings for all popular flies used there.*

BLUE SMOLT

HOOK: *Mustad 9575, Nos. 1-6.*
THREAD: *Black.*
WEIGHT: *12-20 wraps lead wire.*
TAIL: *Silver mylar tubing strands.*
BODY: *Silver mylar tubing tied with fluorescent orange thread.*
THROAT: *Red calf tail.*
UNDERWING: *White bucktail.*
OVERWING: *Blue bucktail.*
TOPPING: *Mallard flank fibers.*

KATMAI SMOLT

HOOK: *Eagle Claw 1197G, Nos. 4-8.*
THREAD: *Black.*
TAIL: *Insect-green floss.*
BUTT: *Peacock herl.*
RIB: *Peacock herl.*
BODY: *Insect-green floss.*
THROAT: *Blue and red hackle fibers, mixed.*
UNDERWING: *Polar bear.*
OVERWING: *Light green bucktail.*
TOPPING: *Peacock herl.*
CHEEKS: *Jungle cock or substitute.*

LITTLE CHINOOK

HOOK: *Mustad 9575, Nos. 2-6.*
THREAD: *Black.*
WEIGHT: *12-20 turns lead wire.*
TAIL: *Silver mylar tubing strands.*
BODY: *Silver mylar tubing tied with orange fluorescent thread.*
THROAT: *Red hackle.*
UNDERWING: *Silver mylar tubing strands.*
OVERWING: *White marabou.*
TOPPING: *Peacock herl.*
SIDE WINGS: *Light blue dyed grizzly hackle.*

SHOWGIRL

HOOK: *Mustad 3407, No. 1/0.*
THREAD: *Fluorescent red.*
WING: *Cerise marabou.*
OVERWING: *Purple flashabou.*
COLLAR: *Purple saddle hackle.*
NOTE: *Marabou shrinks down when wet; use a lot of it on these Alaskabou patterns.*

Saltwater Flies

LEFTY'S DECEIVER, RED/WHITE
HOOK: *Mustad 3407, Nos. 4/0-2.*
THREAD: *Black.*
TAIL: *Six to eight white hackle feathers.*
FLASH: *Six to ten strips medium mylar tinsel.*
BODY: *Wide silver mylar tinsel.*
COLLAR: *White bucktail.*
WING: *Red bucktail.*
TOPPING: *Peacock herl.*

SEA DUCER, RED/WHITE
HOOK: *Mustad 3407, Nos. 2/0-2.*
THREAD: *Red.*
TAIL: *Four to six white hackles.*
FLASH: *Six to ten strands medium mylar tinsel.*
BODY: *White hackle, wound on full.*
HACKLE: *Red.*
NOTE: *A popular variation is tied with yellow saddles for the tail and body, again with a red hackle collar at the front.*

CHICO'S ORANGE/GRIZZLY
HOOK: *Mustad 3407, No. 3/0.*
THREAD: *Fluorescent orange.*
TAIL: *Two orange saddles enveloped by two grizzly saddles.*
HACKLE: *One orange and one grizzly saddle, wound together.*
HEAD: *Fluorescent orange, tied beak style.*

JOE BROOKS BLONDE
HOOK: *Mustad 3407, No. 3/0-2.*
THREAD: *Black.*
TAIL: *Yellow bucktail.*
BODY: *Silver mylar tinsel.*
WING: *Yellow bucktail.*
NOTE: *The Brooks Blonde series is also tied in white, blue, and green. All colors are effective.*

BONEFISH SPECIAL
HOOK: *Mustad 3407, Nos. 1/0-6.*
THREAD: *Red.*
BODY: *Silver tinsel chenille.*
UNDERWING: *Pink bucktail.*
OVERWING: *Grizzly hackles.*
HACKLE: *Pink.*

LEFTY'S DECEIVER, COCKROACH
HOOK: *Mustad 3407, Nos. 4/0-2.*
THREAD: *Black.*
TAIL: *Six to eight grizzly hackles.*
FLASH: *Six to ten strands medium mylar tinsel.*
BODY: *Wide silver mylar tinsel.*
COLLAR: *Brown bucktail.*
NOTE: *There are as many variations of Lefty's Deceiver as there are hackle colors. It is an excellent pattern wherever you fish the salt.*

WHISTLER, RED/WHITE
HOOK: *Mustad 3407, Nos. 3/0-2.*
THREAD: *Red.*
TAIL: *White bucktail.*
WINGS: *Four grizzly hackles.*
BODY: *Red chenille.*
HACKLE: *Red.*
EYES: *Bead chain.*
NOTE: *The Whistler is also tied with yellow bucktail.*

STREAKER
HOOK: *Mustad 3407, No. 3/0.*
THREAD: *Green.*
TAIL: *White bucktail with 10-20 strands silver mylar over top.*
BODY: *Green thread.*
MID-WING: *Green bucktail.*
THROAT: *Green bucktail.*
UNDERWING: *15-20 peacock herl strands.*
OVERWING: *Two matched peacock swords, back to back.*
CHEEKS: *Green bucktail.*

PINK SHRIMP
HOOK: *Mustad 3407, Nos. 3/0-2.*
THREAD: *Pink.*
RIB: *Two pink hackles, palmered.*
BODY: *Pink chenille.*
SHELLBACK AND TAIL: *Pink bucktail.*

CRAZY CHARLIE
HOOK: *Mustad 3407, Nos. 2-8.*
THREAD: *White.*
BODY: *Flat pearl tinsel with 1/32-inch clear Swannundaze over top.*
WING: *White calf tail and pearl flashabou.*
EYES: *Bead chain.*

Lefty's Deceiver, Red/White

Lefty's Deceiver, Cockroach

Sea Ducer, Red/White

Whistler, Red/White

Chico's Orange/Grizzly

Streaker

Joe Brooks Blonde

Pink Shrimp

Bonefish Special

Crazy Charlie

Bass and Panfish Flies

DAHLBERG DIVER
HOOK: *Mustad 37187, Nos. 1/0-10.*
THREAD: *Black.*
HOOK GUARD: *30-lb. monofialment.*
UNDERWING: *Peacock herl and flashabou strands.*
OVERWING: *Olive marabou.*
SIDEWING: *Olive-dyed badger hackles.*
COLLAR: *Black-dyed deer body hair.*
HEAD: *Rear half black deer hair; front half green deer hair.*

DEER HAIR BUG, BLACK/YELLOW
HOOK: *Mustad 36890, Nos. 1/0-10.*
THREAD: *Black.*
TAIL: *Black bucktail.*
BODY: *Deer body hair spun and clipped: black/yellow/black.*
NOTE: *The colors of this bug can be varied to suit your whim.*

HAIR MOUSE
HOOK: *Mustad 3906, Nos. 2/0-6.*
THREAD: *Black.*
TAIL: *Mottled turkey quill.*
BODY: *Natural gray deer body hair, spun and clipped.*
WHISKERS: *Moose mane.*

HAIR FROG
HOOK: *Mustad 3906, Nos. 1/0-6.*
THREAD: *Black.*
LEGS: *Brown and yellowish-green bucktail, mixed, jointed.*
BODY: *Olive deer body hair, spun and clipped.*

BLACK AND WHITE MOTH
HOOK: *Mustad 3906, Nos. 1-6.*
THREAD: *Black.*
TAIL: *Red hackles.*
BODY: *Deer body hair spun and clipped: black/white/black.*
WING: *Black and white bucktail, mixed.*

Dahlberg Diver

Eelworm Streamer

Deer Hair Bug, Black/Yellow

Deer Hair Bug, Natural/White

Hair Mouse

Bubble Pup

Hair Frog

Woolly Leech

Black and White Moth

Jet Bug

EELWORM STREAMER
HOOK: *Mustad 36890, Nos. 1/0-6.*
THREAD: *Red.*
HOOK GUARD: *30-pound monofilament.*
TAIL: *Four black hackles.*
RIB: *Grizzly hackle.*
BODY: *Black yarn or chenille.*
EYES: *Bead chain.*
NOTE: *Color variations of this dressing are only limited by the colors of hackles you own.*

DEER HAIR BUG, NATURAL/WHITE
HOOK: *Mustad 36890, Nos. 1/0-10.*
THREAD: *White.*
TAIL: *Brown bucktail.*
BODY: *Deer body hair spun and clipped: natural/white.*
NOTE: *Tied on long-shank Nos. 12 and 14 hooks, these simple bugs are extremely effective for bluegills and crappies.*

BUBBLE PUP
HOOK: *Mustad 9672, Nos. 2/0-6.*
THREAD: *Black.*
TAIL: *Black hackles.*
COLLAR: *Yellow deer body hair.*
BODY: *Yellow deer body hair, spun and clipped.*
NOTE: *The colors of this dressing can be varied to suit the whim of the tier . . . or of the bass.*

WOOLLY LEECH
HOOK: *Mustad 36890, Nos. 1/0-4.*
THREAD: *Black.*
HOOK GUARD: *30-lb. monofilament.*
TAIL: *Black marabou.*
HACKLE: *Black, palmered.*
BODY: *Black chenille.*
EYES: *Bead chain.*
HOOK: *Another dressing that can be varied in color by substituting for the materials listed.*

JET BUG
HOOK: *Mustad 9674, Nos. 2-8.*
THREAD: *Black.*
BODY: *Deer hair spun and clipped.*
WHISKERS: *Moose mane.*
BACK AND TAIL: *Moose mane.*